Evelyn Findlater's concern with healthy eating began when she ran a wholefood shop and restaurant in Devon for three years. So many customers asked her for recipes and tips that she started to give classes, and subsequently wrote her first book, *Wholefood Cookery Course* (1983). She has given seminars to home economist teachers in schools and run courses for school meals supervisors, and has also appeared in a television series. She now devotes her time to cookery writing.

Making Your Own Home Proteins

Tofu, Tempeh, Soft Cheeses, Yoghurt and Sprouted Seeds

Evelyn Findlater

CENTURY PUBLISHING
LONDON

First published in Great Britain in 1985
by Century Publishing Co. Ltd,
Portland House
12-13 Greek Street, London W1V 5LE
Reprinted 1985

ISBN 0 7126 0817 6

Printed in Great Britain in 1985 by
Hunt Barnard Printing Ltd, Aylesbury, Bucks.

ৰঙ Contents ইৰ

Sprouting Seeds 120; How to Grow Your own
Bean, Grain and Seed Sprouts 122; Recipes Using
Bean, Grain and Seed Sprouts 125

⋅⋅⋅ *Introduction* ⋅⋅⋅

Writing this book has been one of the most rewarding experiences in my cookery career so far. I have learnt so much from my own experiments and from others who have developed a greater understanding and knowledge about the food we eat. No longer for me is food just something we eat because we are hungry or make fancy for special occasions. Yes, I still do both of those things but what has become more important to me now is how it grows and how it is produced.

I remember the first time I made a perfect 450g/1lb rectangle of tofu I felt as if I had performed a miracle. Seeing my soya beans change over hours to become tempeh and harvesting a huge variety of fresh, live bean and seed sprouts without needing a garden or digging the soil gives me a greater satisfaction creatively and a deeper awareness of all growing things.

If anyone had described to me just 10 years ago what I would be cooking and eating today I would not have believed them. Most of the foods mentioned in the book were completely unknown to me then. I had tested a very strong goat's cheese in France which coloured my attitude to all goat's milk products for years. In a Chinese restaurant I had eaten soggy bean sprouts and wobbly cubes of something floating in a soup which I now know was tofu, without being the least bit impressed or stimulated to find out what exactly these foods were.

Around this time health food stores were also unknown

territory although they greatly intrigued me. Occasionally I would buy some natural yoghurt, packets of cereal and the odd bag of lentils for soup but the rest remained a mystery. It was not until I went to college as a mature student teacher that I came into contact with people who actually ate brown rice and beans and discussed ecological problems about famine and the misuse of land given over to livestock for the over-production of meat, that I began to find out more and decided to experiment with alternative proteins. Literature in this area was very scarce then and my efforts were not always rewarded, but whatever I read on the subject of healthier eating encouraged me to keep trying. Fortunately I love cooking, so even though I ruined a few dishes, I was quite excited by new foods. My shelves with jars of different coloured beans, nuts and seeds and more of a variety of herbs and spices were a constant stimulous. This did not mean my collection of gourmet and traditional cookery books was discarded, indeed, I am most grateful to these writers. The good ones encouraged my natural desire to create in the kitchen.

At this time I had three children, aged 11, 9 and 3 years so I had to tread very lightly with changes in our family diet. I introduced new foods by incorporating them with what was our usual fare, not without a few clashes I might add. Gradually the refined foods were replaced by more natural foods. Beans in traditional-type dishes were accepted and pizzas looked and tasted more alive with sesame seeds in the wholemeal base. In fact, within a year the kids started to comment on how taste-less certain foods were that had previously been the norm for them.

Through the years I have read avidly about the eating habits of other cultures around the globe and come to realise how much we in the West have neglected what we once knew and have not developed very far beyond the meat and two veg. The more I read the more conscious I became of what we should be eating, not just for our own personal health, but for the well-being of the earth, which we seem to take too much from, and for the millions who do not have enough to eat.

Whether you eat meat or not, a good diet is one that is balanced. We all have similar nutritional requirements which include the right amount of protein and unprocessed carbohydrates and an adequate supply of vitamins and minerals. But research has revealed that our Western diet is low in fibre, overloaded with saturated fats, sugar and salt, not to mention additives, and concludes that these factors have become an increasing threat to our health. Many people are under the misapprehension that those of us who advocate a healthy diet are vegetarian and do not approve of meat-eating either because of moral or health reasons or both. Well my experience is that many healthy eaters gradually begin to enjoy a varied diet, consequently eat less meat, experiment with other forms of protein and feel better for it. When you become involved with thinking about health and diet you are forced to think beyond convenience and habit. There is one very important factor to be aware of regarding meat eating and this is that unfortunately most of our meat comes from animals which are factory farmed and injected with hormones. The meat, eggs and milk from them thus contains residual amounts of these hormones. Opinions vary as to whether these residues affect the human body but we wouldn't think twice about rejecting a contaminated bag of flour, so why do we accept unnaturally produced livestock? This is a very controversial subject but one that deserves our attention at a time when land is scarce, many people are starving and about ten times more land is needed to rear a cow than to grow its protein equivalent in the vegetable kingdom, the soya bean.

You can buy tofu, both the firm and silken varieties mentioned in this book, quite easily from most health food stores. Goat's milk products are becoming more easily available in those same shops as well as canned gluten. Unfortunately tempeh, which is sold in America, is not yet available in this country but from information I have received it might be obtainable in the near future. Bean sprouts of course are sold in supermarkets and greengrocers but generally only the Chinese mung bean sprouts.

But whatever might be available I hope this book encourages you to experiment with these proteins and incorporate them in your everyday diet. I also hope that you gain the joy that I have found, not only in tasting, but in creating simple, cheap and nourishing foods that strengthen the body and do not strain the earth's resources.

CHAPTER I
❧ *The Soya Dairy* ❧

The very first soya dairy was started in Shanghai in 1936 by an American, Dr Harry Miller. Up until that time tofu was one of the staple foods of the Chinese people, but the milk was mostly used to produce tofu and not widely drunk as a nutritious beverage. Unfortunately, after a few months of hard work, which achieved a widespread demand for soya milk throughout the city of Shanghai, the plant was destroyed in a bomb raid. Dr Miller was well aware of the high nutritional and ecological value of soya products, which make efficient use of land and enable more people to be better fed than is possible with the rearing of cattle for milk production or meat-eating. Although he did not succeed in spreading his ideas widely in America when he returned there after the bomb disaster, his efforts stimulated a desire, which is growing rapidly today, to preserve the world we live in and make better use of a wider variety of wholesome foods.

For several years after I had changed our family diet to a more healthy way of eating I avoided using the soya bean. My first experience of tasting it was in one of those 'really healthy soups' where everything 'good for you' was thrown in. It was ghastly! I ended up with chronic wind and sadly an aversion to this marvellous food. Fortunately as my interest in cooking for health grew, so did my interest in nutrition and ecology. That first failure began to challenge me as I read about strange foods like tofu, miso and tempeh and 'the complete protein bean'. I started to experiment and now nine years later the soya bean with all its versatility is very much part of our diet.

I include the recipe for tofu (soya cheese) in all my cookbooks because it is a complete protein food of the vegetable kingdom and very useful for those on a vegan diet which does not include animal produce in any form.

A complete protein food is one that contains all the essential amino acids that the body needs to build protein. Our bodies require a constant supply of protein as it is not storable like fats. Not only does the body need protein but it must be what is termed 'complete protein'. If not enough is consumed, the body will not grow properly. There are approximately 22 known amino acids necessary for the healthy growth of all body tissues including muscles, blood, skin, hair, nails and internal organs such as the brain, heart, liver and kidneys. Fourteen are produced by the body and the other eight – the essential amino acids – must be obtained from your diet. Meat, fish, dairy produce and the soya bean contain these essential acids.

Extensive research has revealed that although such foods as whole grains, legumes (dried peas, beans and lentils) and nuts and seeds are deficient in some of the essential acids a correct balance can be achieved by complementing these foods in various ways. Combining grains with legumes, grains with nuts and seeds, grains with dairy produce, or legumes with nuts and seeds in the right proportions will give you sufficient complete protein. A guideline to these proportions is to serve approximately 50 per cent grains (remember most grains treble in size when cooked) with 25 per cent legumes, nuts and seeds or dairy produce and 25 per cent fresh land or sea vegetables. The majority of diets throughout the world do include meat and fish, but these items are not essential as long as the protein consumed is balanced and complete. Using the soya bean makes this a simpler task.

Another important point, especially for those on a vegan diet, is that vitamin B12, which is essential for the functioning of all body cells, is only rarely found in the plant world. Sources of B12 include meat and all dairy produce, eggs, sprouted soya beans and other sprouted seeds, tempeh (a fermented soya bean food, see pages 49–50 for how to make), seaweed and comfrey if grown on soil rich in this vitamin. A deficiency of B12 can cause anaemia and even more serious damage to the central nervous system which can be fatal. A vegetarian diet which includes dairy produce will supply adequate B12.

The Soya Bean

The soya bean is approximately 38 per cent protein, equal to that of beef. Unlike meat, however, it contains unsaturated fat and a high level of lecithin which reduces the level of cholesterol in the blood, thus lessening the possibility of heart attack. The soya bean is also an alkaline food which corrects acidity in the body and it is the cheapest source of minerals and 'complete protein' available today.

A one-acre harvest of this wonderful bean will provide enough protein for one human being for six years. The harvest from the same amount of land fed to animals will yield only enough protein for one human being for approximately 80 days. What better reason for experimenting with this 'miracle bean' by making some of the delicious, highly nutritious foods which are traditional in Chinese, Japanese and Indonesian cuisine and will add an exciting dimension to your diet?

It is important to note that proper soaking and cooking of pulses (dried peas and beans) is vital because they all contain to a greater or lesser degree substances such as glycosides, saponides and alkaloids which are harmful to digestion. This applies even more so to the soya bean which contains a trypsin inhibitor that prevents the body assimilating an important amino acid called methionine. The bean, the flour from the bean and sprouted soya beans must be cooked to render these substances harmless. I soak pulses, except lentils or mung beans, for 12 hours, changing the soaking water three times. Then I rinse them well, boil them in fresh water for 10 minutes and simmer for 40 minutes to one hour.

Soya beans need even more soaking and cooking time than other legumes. Soak them for 15 hours in summer time and about 20 to 24 hours in winter time, changing the water 3 to 4 times. Rinse them afterwards and boil them vigorously in fresh water for 10 minutes, then simmer for approximately 3 hours. If using a pressure cooker, the beans will only take 30 minutes to cook, but they must be pre-soaked for the same amount of time.

Products of the Soya Bean

Soya Flour
Soya bean flour has even greater nutritional value than the beans themselves. It is highly concentrated and contains no gluten, so it is great for those on a gluten-free diet. It makes a marvellous creamy white sauce and is a useful and healthy thickener for soups and stews. As well as thickening, it adds concentrated protein. I sometimes add it to my flour when bread making (see page 135).

Shoyu and Tamari (Naturally Fermented Soy Sauce)
There are many brands of soy sauce on the market. Most are synthetically compounded with additives such as caramel and syrup to give colour and flavour. These products are to be avoided; although they are cheaper to manufacture as they are made within a few days, they do not produce the protein yield of the naturally fermented soy sauces, shoyu and tamari.

Traditionally, the method of producing the natural sauce is to ferment the beans in vats with water, roasted cracked wheat and natural salt for one to three years. This fermentation process produces a source of vitamin B12, the one vitamin which is thought to be non-existent in a diet of plants alone. Further, the combination of grains with soya beans increases the protein yield, while the fermentation process itself enables our bodies to utilise the protein more efficiently. Added to this, when the natural sauce is added to other foods such as whole grains, nuts, seeds and beans, it increases the amount of protein that can be digested.

Miso

A wonder food! I don't say that flippantly, because just two good teaspoons (10 ml) of miso will give you enough complete protein for one day. How about that! So many of our fellow humans starve and the answer to feeding the poor millions need not be so very difficult.

Miso is a soya bean paste produced by lactic fermentation. The process is lengthy, during which the culture is added to cooked soya beans and cooked rice. Salt is gradually added until the mixture achieves a paste-like consistency. The paste comes in various shades. The darker miso contains up to 90 per cent soya bean while the lighter miso contains more rice and thus less protein. Not only is miso a high protein food but it is also free of cholesterol; it is an aid to digestion, is claimed to help develop a strong resistance to disease and, the most incredible yet substantiated claim of all is that it can remove radioactive substances from the body.

Cooking with Miso

Don't cook it, or at least let it simmer for only one minute in your soup or casserole. Cooking destroys the culture and flavour. Also very important is not just to dollop a lump of miso into your prepared meal. Mix the miso with a little of the hot stock or some warm water to a smooth paste, then stir this with a fork into the prepared food. Remember that miso is salty and it is not necessary to include salt in any dish to which you will be adding miso.

How do I use miso? Well, I have found miso a fantastic tonic. Cook or no cook, and I am one of those people who feels somehow they must feed the world around them – I do nevertheless have off days when I just do not want to prepare anything. Here's my recipe for a good quick tonic.

Simple Miso Tonic
Liquidise two grated carrots in 200 ml/7 fl oz of hot water and stir in 5 ml/1 tsp of miso. Your body will feel better within minutes. That is my experience. Take the tonic twice daily on off-days.

Other recipes for miso are not necessary. I simply use it as an extra protein booster and always in vegetable soups or less complete protein bean stews. (When I say vegetable soups, I mean hearty ones with root vegetables, not leek or asparagus based soups, as miso is strong tasting and would destroy the delicate flavour of these vegetables.)

Soya Milk

Soya milk is low in calories, low in saturated fats and has no cholesterol or sodium (salt). It contains more iron and slightly more protein than cow's milk, with equal amounts of the B vitamins. It is also easy to digest and has an alkaline reaction in the body. For those who have a lactose intolerance or allergy to cow's milk it is invaluable.

Of course mother's milk is by far the best for infant feeding, but for various reasons this is not always available. In such circumstances medically approved infant soya milk formulas are available and will give your child a healthy substitute. After three months of feeding my last child, sadly my milk rapidly decreased. As we were running our wholefood shop and café at the time I assume it was through lack of rest. Even so, at the age of four she is healthy, active and bright, having been put on soya milk and goat's milk to which I added a very little brewers' yeast. I am not, however, an authority on this subject so I feel it is safest to suggest you buy an approved infant formula.

You can use soya milk in any recipe where cow's or goat's milk is called for. It makes delicious sauces, custards and milk shakes, and is great chilled with just a dash of honey. It will also make very good yoghurt (see pages 19–19 for recipe) using the same culture as for goat's milk yoghurt.

Last, but not least, home produced soya milk is less than one third the price of cow's milk and one fifth the price of goat's milk. One pound (455g) soya beans yields approximately 7 pints (4 litres) of milk.

Tofu

Tofu is a high quality complete protein-rich food, a good source of minerals such as iron and calcium. It contains potassium, phosphorous and a good supply of the B and E vitamins. It is also low in sodium (salt) compared to meat and all dairy produce and has approximately a quarter of the calories to be found in an equal portion of meat. Tofu has no cholesterol and is low in saturated fats, both of which in excess have been found to be contributory factors in heart disease.

Most protein foods have an acid reaction in the body whereas tofu has an alkaline effect. Although tofu has only one third of the protein of meat, what is more important where all protein is concerned is its Net Protein Utilisation, NUP. The protein content might well be high in a particular food before it is eaten but if there are inhibiting factors, which make it difficult to digest, then the body is not able to benefit fully from that high percentage of protein. (For more information on the soya bean and its derivatives it would be well worth your while to read *Diet for a Small Planet* by Frances Moore Lappe.) Surprisingly, research has revealed that the NUP of tofu is actually higher than chicken and just slightly lower than beef.

Again because of the research put in by Frances Moore

Lappe we know that although tofu is a complete protein, its NUP can be increased by combining it with whole grains and, to make a balanced meal, adding it to fresh or lightly cooked vegetables, using it as a spread with herbs and garlic on wholemeal bread or as a stuffing for pitta bread. I also sometimes use it in lasagne instead of curd or Ricotta cheese. My favourite way is to add it to stir-fried vegetables with sweet and sour sauce.

Before I give you what I hope will be some delicious-tasting recipes using soya milk and tofu, I must mention that there is a high fibre food which is the residue of the whole process in making your tofu to be made good use of. This is the pulp left after you have squeezed all the milk from the beans. It is called okara. Besides being high in fibre it contains 3·5 per cent protein which is similar to the amount in unskimmed milk. It can be used in the toppings of fruit crumbles and in granola (toasted muesli). I also use it in bean or nut burger mixtures instead of breadcrumbs or bulgur (pre-cooked cracked wheat).

Last but not least, don't throw away the whey which trickles gently from your tofu press as the curds are moulded together into a smooth firm or silken soya cheese. It contains some protein and B vitamins and the natural sugar of the soya bean. This natural sugar content helps yeast to rise more quickly in bread-making and the result is a much lighter loaf, which is slightly sweet, yet does not contain ordinary sugar. It's delicious in soups! It's great even as a cleaning agent as it breaks down fats and grease, so you can even wash the dishes with it. For this you will only need about half a cupful to a bowl of hot water. I couldn't believe how well it cleans the first time I tried it out.

So, all in all making tofu is very exciting but, even if the process is too daunting for some of you, now at least when you buy tofu you will know what a wonderful food it is and maybe one day when circumstances arise, you will have a go at producing your own.

How to Make Soya Milk and Tofu (Soya Cheese)

Read all the instructions carefully and have everything ready before you start

You can make tofu with Epsom salts or lemon juice, but I find the best results, a higher yield and greater firmness, are achieved by using nigari. Rich in minerals, nigari is the residue left after the salt (sodium chloride) and water are removed from sea water. The residue is sun-dried and bought as crystals. I also use a Japanese tofu press which is made from Japanese cypress wood (iroki). Both nigari and the tofu press can be obtained by mail order from the address on page 146. The press comes with a sachet of nigari and full instructions but it is best to follow my instructions as they give you the exact amount of water to use, which is most important. The quantities given make approximately 450 g/1 lb of firm tofu.

Soya milk

350 g/12 oz dry weight soya beans
10 ml/2 teaspoon nigari,
  dissolved in 1 200 ml-teacup
  of warm water
or
15 ml/3 teaspoon Epsom salts,
  dissolved in 1 200 ml-teacup of

warm water or
90 ml/6 tablespoon lemon juice
  dissolved in 1 200 ml-teacup of
  warm water (this will give you
  a tangy, slightly coarse tofu,
  quite tasty)

1. Wash and soak the soya beans for 24 hours. Change the water three times during soaking.
2. Rinse the beans well after soaking and to each cup of soaked beans add 1 cup of boiling water. Using a food processor or liquidiser, blend cup by cup. Leave the motor on for 1½

minutes each time to achieve a reasonably smooth, runny batter consistency.

3. Grease a large, heavy-bottomed pan big enough to take about 5 litres/10 pints of liquid.

4. Bring 8 cups of fresh water to the boil and pour in the liquidised bean purée. Bring to the boil, stirring constantly. Keep on moderate heat only to prevent burning. Once boiling, turn down the heat and leave to simmer for 20 minutes. The mixture will be frothy, so spoon back some of the froth to make sure that the liquid is gently bubbling underneath. Stir occasionally.

5. Dissolve the nigari in the water (or the Epsom salts or lemon juice) to make your solidifier.

6. Stretch a straining bag or good sized piece of muslin over a colander, leaving plenty hanging over for tying up. Place the colander over a large clean bowl to catch the milk.

7. Put on rubber gloves and pour the boiled bean liquid into the straining bag or muslin. The soya milk will filter through.

8. Rinse the cooking pot with 1 cup of boiling water and add this to the straining bag. Twist the bag or cloth tightly and squeeze out as much milk as possible.

9. Open the bag and pour in three more 200 ml-teacups of boiling water, tie up and squeeze again. The soya milk is now ready.

The milk will freeze well after it is cooled. The quicker you cool the milk, the longer it will keep, so if you don't want to make tofu, cool it by immersing the bowl in a sink of cold water, changing the water as it warms. Soya milk will keep fresh in the refrigerator for up to four days. Frozen, it will be good for at least 3 months.

Tofu

1. Rinse out the cooking pot, pour the hot soya milk back into it and reheat. The milk must reach at least 85°C/185°F, so bring it to just under boiling point. (Note: if using Epsom salts, 74°C/165°F is hot enough.)

2. After it is hot, remove from the heat and add your chosen solidifier by stirring briskly, while *slowly* pouring in one-third of the nigari, Epsom salts or lemon juice liquid. Continue to stir for half a minute, making sure you stir in milk from the sides and bottom of the pan.

3. Let the movement of the liquid stop then using the back of your stirring spoon, pour a further third of the solidifier on to the surface of the milk. Cover and leave for 3 minutes, then stir again.

4. Using the back of the spoon, trickle the remaining solidifier over the surface of the milk, then slowly and gently stir only about 1 cm/½ in of the surface of the milk as you count to 20. Cover and leave for another 3 minutes, then uncover and stir the liquid. You should now have a mixture of curds and whey. The curds will be cream-coloured and the whey a clear yellow colour.

5. Line the tofu press with a clean piece of muslin, draping it over the edge as it will be folded over the tofu later. If you have no press just place the cloth over a colander which is on top of a bowl to catch the whey.

6. Ladle the curds and whey into the press or colander. The curds will stay in the cloth and the whey will drip through. The tofu will be quite soft at this stage.

7. Fold the cloth over the tofu, place the lid of the press on top (or a small plate if you are using a colander) and a weight on top of this. The weight should be about 1 kg/2 lb. Leave to stand for 20-30 minutes. This will give you a firm tofu which is easy to slice. Uncover the tofu.

To keep in the refrigerator, fill a bowl with cold water and ease the tofu into this. Change the water every day and it will last for 6 days. You can freeze it, but the texture alters and it is then only good for soups and stews.

You can now purchase firm or silken (soft) tofu in health stores or wholefood and Chinese shops. If you find it difficult to obtain in your locality, see page 140 for the best brand name and address for mail orders.

Silken Tofu

A word here about silken tofu which is sometimes suggested for certain recipes such as salad dressings or light puddings. I prefer to buy silken tofu as the whole process of making firm, solid tofu takes some time. Might I suggest you try Paul's Silken Tofu which can now be purchased in many wholefood shops and health stores or by mail order (see address on page 140). His firm tofu is also excellent to try out my recipes with if you have never eaten tofu before.

To make silken tofu, you simply make a rich soya milk which has approximately 850 ml/1½ pints less water (4½ cups) and half the coagulant than for making regular soya milk and firm tofu. You then keep the curds and whey together, pour them into a bowl and let them cool. This produces a considerably larger quantity of soft tofu as the curds and whey are not separated. You can freeze this in several containers and defrost as required for blended dishes.

Yuba

Yuba is the name for the skin which develops on top of soya milk when it is heating, similar to the skin which forms on cow's or goat's milk. In China and Japan yuba is considered a delicacy and can be bought either fresh or dried. It is a very nutritious high energy food which contains at least 50 per cent protein, is rich in minerals, unsaturated oils and natural sugars. It is a great food for babies mixed with fruit purées, for pregnant and nursing mothers and of course for all sportsmen and women. A few spoonfuls of this high energy food will not only set a runner on his/her way but provide valuable nutrients which dextrose tablets do not.

It is very simple to make and dry. A double boiler is useful but you can use a shallow saucepan placed over a pan of hot water over low heat. This is necessary because the yuba takes approximately 8 minutes to form and the milk has to be kept at a steady temperature of about 79°C/175°F. A cooking thermometer is necessary to test the temperature. The best yield is obtained by using a rich soya milk. To make that you simply use 4 200-ml cups of water less when making the soya milk (see pages 13–14).

How to Make Yuba

1. Pour soya milk into the saucepan to a level of about 5 cm/2 in and heat to a temperature of 79°C/175°F. Do not boil. Keep on heat until a thick skin forms. This takes approximately 8 minutes.
2. Cut the skin with a sharp knife all round the edge then lift it up carefully by sliding a long thick knitting needle or chopstick under the middle.
3. Top up milk to the 5 cm/2 in level and repeat the process until you have several sheets of yuba.
4. If you wish to dry the yuba, hang it until it is brittle.

Freshly made yuba is delicious either as a savoury spread or as a sweet dish mixed with fruit. My favourite way of eating it is adding a few fresh chopped mixed herbs, black pepper or paprika, a little sea salt and a touch of garlic. Spread on wholemeal toast or used for open sandwiches with sliced red pepper it makes a truly delicious and healthy tummy-filler.

The dried variety can be stored in the refrigerator for several weeks. It is great chopped up in soups and added to stir-fried vegetables and rice dishes because of its high protein content.

Soya Milk Yoghurt

You can make yoghurt out of soya milk in exactly the same way as you would using goat's or cow's milk. The same culture starter, lactobacillus bulgarious, is used. (For more information on the nutritional value of yoghurt see page 95.)

You can buy a yoghurt-making kit or use wide-rimmed thermos flasks to keep your yoghurt at the right temperature, but I use preserving jars which I incubate in the airing cupboard at around the temperature of 43°C/110°F, just above body temperature.

For perfection, when testing the temperature of the milk before adding the culture, it is best to have a dairy thermometer which floats on the surface of the liquid. You can use a jam-making thermometer which can be bought from most chemists but you have to hold it in the liquid until the right temperature is reached. If you are using the finger test then the milk should still feel warm but not burn your finger.

The best soya milk yoghurt is achieved by using a thick soya milk (see recipe for making soya milk and tofu on pages 13–16.) Follow all instructions for the milk but use 850 ml/1 ½ pints less water.

How to Make Soya Milk Yoghurt

It is important to sterilise containers and equipment. Do this by immersing the clean, inverted jars into a pot of water (caps as well) plus a tablespoon and a plastic fork or spatula, which is useful for stirring in the culture. Bring to boil and boil for a few minutes. If using a commercial dry culture then follow directions on the packet, but if using a good brand of natural yoghurt then you will need 2 tablespoons for every quart of milk. So, filling, say, 4 preserving jars which hold 285 ml/½ pint each you will need to stir in 1 dessertspoon of natural yoghurt in each jar when the milk is at the right temperature.

1. Bring 1.1 litres/2 pints of soya milk to boil, hold for ½ minute stirring constantly.
2. Pour 285 ml/½ pint into the hot sterilised jars, cover and let the milk cool to 43°C/110°F. To test without a dairy- or jam-making thermometer, the milk is ready when the jars feel comfortably hot to your wrist but not burning.
3. Spoon 1 dessertspoon of natural yoghurt into each jar. Stir briskly with a plastic fork or spatula, cover and leave to stand in the airing cupboard or suitable warm place for 3 to 4 hours or until set. Check the temperature with a room thermometer because the culture needs a constant temperature of around 43°C/110°F to grow properly.
4. When set, refrigerate.

How to Make Soya Milk Yoghurt Cheese

1.1 litres/2 pints yoghurt yields approximately 340 g/12 oz thick, creamy cheese. It is delicious for making cheesecake mixed with tofu and lemon (see pages 41–2 for recipe.) You can also use it in salad dressings (see pages 37–40) instead of tofu, but you will need a little less lemon juice as the yoghurt does not have the bland flavour of tofu.

All you need is a piece of muslin and some cord to tie up the dripping yoghurt.

1. Spread the muslin over a colander, pour the fresh yoghurt into this, twist and tie the edges with the cord and hang over a pot and let drip for 4 hours. This will give you a soft cheese but for a firmer, thick creamy cheese let drip overnight.

The soft yoghurt cheese is great on baked potatoes topped with chives, paprika, a pinch of sea salt and freshly ground black pepper.

The firmer cheese is lovely mixed with herbs, seasoning and small chopped salad vegetables similar to the 'Tofu Dip Delight' recipe on pages 40–1 and as previously mentioned for making cheesecake.

Both soft and firmer yoghurt cheese mix well with fresh and dried soaked fruit, toasted nuts and a little honey to sweeten if needed.

Recipes using Tofu and Soya Milk

I usually marinate, coat and sauté pieces of tofu (see first recipe) before adding it to casseroles, stir-fried vegetables or vegetable sauces like Italian tomato sauce or sweet and sour sauce. It is delicious cut into small cubes and added to soups at the end of cooking time or just crumbled in dishes like lasagne instead of curd or Ricotta cheese. I also love it as a topping for pizza with pumpkin seeds sprinkled over it (see pages 33–5 for recipe). Its uses are endless, so have a go with these recipes and I hope they will encourage you to experiment for yourself with this wonderful food.

Savoury Sautéed Tofu
Serves 4

340 g/12 oz firm tofu
45 ml/3 tablespoons shoyu
  (naturally fermented soya sauce)
85 g/3 oz wholemeal flour, plain
1 large clove garlic, crushed with a
  pestle and mortar with ½
  teaspoon sea salt or

½ teaspoon garlic salt
freshly ground black pepper
1 rounded teaspoon sweet mixed
  herbs
sunflower, corn or sesame seed oil
  for frying

1. Cut tofu into 2 cm/¾ in cubes.
2. Sprinkle half the shoyu in a large shallow bowl and place the tofu cubes on to this and pour the rest of the shoyu on top.
3. Let marinate for a few minutes while you prepare the other ingredients.
4. Mix flour with garlic and salt, or garlic salt, pepper and mixed herbs, in a shallow bowl.
5. Shake off excess soya sauce from the tofu pieces and dip each one, coating well, in the flour mixture.
6. Heat 6 mm/¼ in of oil in a frying pan and fry the tofu, turning it until golden brown on all sides.
7. Drain on absorbent kitchen paper and keep warm in a low heated oven until needed, or cool if using in a salad.

Pot Barley and Tofu Soup

This delicious, hearty, warming soup with the addition of tofu
and accompanied by wholemeal pitta bread stuffed with salad
will provide a wholesome lunch or supper dish for four people.
Use pot barley which is the whole grain. Pearl barley is
polished, with all the fibre and most of the germ removed.
Instead of the savoury sautéed tofu you can simply chop up firm
tofu and add as directed.

*340 g/12 oz, 2 cm/¾ in cubes of
savoury sautéed tofu, see page
21 for recipe.*

85 g/3 oz pot barley

850 ml/1½ pints water

3 tablespoons sunflower oil

*1 large onion, peeled and finely
chopped*

2 cloves garlic, crushed

*3 medium sized carrots, scraped
and cut into 1 cm/½ in sticks*

*2 medium sized potatoes, cut into
small cubes*

3 sticks celery, finely chopped

1 level tablespoon tomato purée

*1 rounded teaspoon basil or mixed
herbs*

1 bay leaf

*2 tablespoons fresh parsley,
chopped (when available)*

*450 g/1 lb soft, ripe tomatoes,
skinned and finely chopped, or
canned tomatoes*

*1 level tablespoon miso (soya bean
paste)*

*1 tablespoon shoyu (naturally
fermented soya sauce)*

freshly ground black pepper

1. Wash barley well and soak in the water either overnight or
   for at least four hours.
2. Drain and reserve the liquid, topping it up to a level of
   850 ml/1½ pints.
3. Heat oil in a large heavy based saucepan and sauté the
   onion and garlic for 5 minutes with the lid on.
4. Add carrots, potatoes, celery and drained barley.
5. Stir in the basil or mixed herbs, bay leaf and parsley and
   continue to fry for 3 minutes only.
6. Add the chopped tomatoes and the tomato purée and barley
   soaking water.

7. Bring to boil and simmer gently for 20 minutes. Take off heat.
8. Mix a few tablespoons of the hot soup with the miso to make a runny batter consistency and stir this into the rest of the soup, blending well together.
9. Finally, stir in the tofu cubes, shoyu and pepper and heat through just before serving.

For children who pick out vegetables or old people who find it difficult to chew, this soup is even tastier when liquidised, but you might have to add a little more water as the soup will be quite thick.

Leek and Watercress Soup with Tofu
Serves 6/8 (small portions)

This is a very delicate flavoured soup with thin rings of leek and chopped watercress cooked for just ten minutes. As in the previous recipe you can use the savoury sautéed tofu or, as I prefer because of the light flavour, small cubes of plain unsautéed tofu.

1 litre/1 ¼ pints water
1 ½ vegetable stock cubes or 2 level teaspoons herb salt
2 medium sized leeks, trimmed, washed and cut into thin rings
115 g/4 oz small button mushrooms, sliced

1 bunch watercress, chopped (use stems)
225 g/8 oz firm tofu cut into small cubes or Savoury Sautéed Tofu (see page 21)
freshly ground black pepper to taste

1. Bring water to boil with stock cubes or sea salt. Add leek rings and simmer with lid on for 5 minutes only.
2. Add mushroom slices and continue to simmer for 3 more minutes.

3. Add chopped watercress, tofu and black pepper. Simmer for
a few more minutes until the tofu is warm right through.
Serve immediately, piping hot in small bowls.

Vegetable Casserole with Tofu
Serves 4

This very simple, tasty casserole can also be a filling for a
vegetable and tofu pie. Just place the mixture in a pie dish and
top with wholemeal pastry (for wholemeal pastry see pages
35–6) and bake for 30 minutes at 190°C/375°F/Gas 5.

1 large onion, chopped
1 large clove garlic, crushed
2 medium carrots, scraped and cut
   into thin 2.5 cm/1 in sticks
3 tablespoons sunflower oil
3 sticks celery, chopped
1 medium sized green pepper, cut
   into small pieces
1 tablespoon fresh chopped parsley
1 teaspoon mixed herbs

1 tablespoon wholemeal flour or
   unbleached white flour
½ vegetable stock cube dissolved in
   600 ml/1 pint hot water
1 generous tablespoon tomato purée
1 cup frozen peas
1 tablespoon shoyu (naturally
   fermented soya sauce)
340 g/12 oz Savoury Sautéed
   Tofu (see page 21 for recipe)

1. Sauté the onion, garlic and carrot in the oil for 5 minutes
   only.
2. Add celery and continue to sauté for 3 more minutes.
3. Stir in the green pepper, parsley, mixed herbs and fry for 2
   more minutes.
4. Stir in the flour and cook, stirring constantly, for
   ½ minute.
5. Add the water (in which you have dissolved the ½ stock
   cube plus the tomato purée) and stir with the peas for 1
   minute more.
6. Stir in the shoyu.

7. Place this mixture into a casserole dish, cover and bake at 190°C/375°F/Gas 5 for 25 minutes.
8. Fork in the tofu and bake for a further 5 minutes until the tofu is warmed through.

Serve with either a whole grain or potatoes steamed in their jackets.

Tofu Risotto
Serves 5

This Rich Italian Sauce with tofu, stirred into brown rice makes a truly nourishing and delightful meal.

340 g/12 oz dry weight Italian short or long grain brown rice

1 level teaspoon sea salt

For the Sauce

3 tablespoons olive or sunflower oil
1 large onion, peeled and finely chopped
2 large cloves garlic, crushed
2 sticks celery, finely chopped (tender stalks)
2 medium sized courgettes, cut into thin rings
½ red and ½ green pepper, cut into small pieces
115 g/4 oz button mushrooms, thinly sliced
1 large bay leaf
1 rounded teaspoon dried basil or

1 tablespoon fresh basil
½ teaspoon tarragon
450 g/1 lb fresh ripe tomatoes, skinned and chopped, or canned tomatoes
1 tablespoon tomato purée
1 tablespoon lemon juice
1 to 2 tablespoons shoyu (naturally fermented soya sauce) (taste after 1 tablespoon)
freshly ground black pepper to taste
340 g/12 oz Savoury Sautéed Tofu (see page 21)

1. Measure out rice in cupfuls while dry. Wash well by placing in a sieve and letting cold water run through the grains for 1 minute.

2. Place in a medium sized heavy-based saucepan with a tight lid.
3. For the Italian rice which is in this recipe, add twice the volume of water to rice. Sprinkle in the salt, bring to boil, turn down to simmer, cover and let simmer for 35 minutes. The water should all be absorbed and the grains separate. (Do not stir or take off lid during cooking time.) While rice is cooking, prepare the sauce.

Rich Italian Sauce

1. Heat oil in a large heavy-based saucepan and sauté onion and garlic for 6 minutes, with lid on.
2. Add celery and continue to sauté for 4 more minutes with lid on.
3. Add courgettes, pepper and mushrooms, this time stirring the vegetables for 2 minutes.
4. Add bay leaf, basil, tarragon and pepper and simmer for one minute. Add the skinned chopped tomatoes, purée, shoyu and lemon juice. Mix well. Heat through, stirring constantly.
5. Place the savoury sautéed tofu on top of the sauce, cover and keep on low heat until tofu is warmed through.

Finally, fork in the cooked rice. Serve with either a fresh green salad or steamed green vegetable such as steamed broccoli, French beans or runner beans.

Bolognese Sauce

The Rich Italian Sauce for the previous recipe makes the base for a lovely Bolognese Sauce for either wholemeal spaghetti or buckwheat spaghetti (which is a very thin, light pasta that contains rutic acid which is good for the circulation and has a delicious nutty flavour).

I simply chop the vegetables up as fine as possible, which cuts down the cooking time, leave out the tarragon, add 2 table-spoons of fresh chopped parsley and double the amount of tomatoes (a 794 g/1 lb 12 oz can will do) and tomato purée. Follow the frying instructions and simmer the sauce for 30 minutes more, adding the tofu 5 minutes before the end of cooking time, with lid slightly off so that some of the tomato juice evaporates and you have a thick, rich sauce.

Tofu Tempura with Sweet and Sour Sauce
Serves 5

Tempura is the Japanese name for deep-fried battered vege-tables, meat or fish. (In India these are called pakora.) The batter can be made with wholemeal flour or unbleached white, but I prefer the delicate taste and resulting texture achieved by using a mixture of gram flour (chick pea flour), brown rice flour and soya flour. By using a polyunsaturated oil with a high 'smoke' point and heating it up well, you make sure the tempura absorbs the minimum amount of fat.

For a healthy starter choose a selection of vegetables such as thin slices of carrot, broccoli florets, small, whole button mushrooms, French beans, and onion, aubergine and peppers cut in thin rings. Dip in the batter, deep fry, drain on kitchen paper and serve hot sprinkled with shoyu (naturally fermented soya sauce) and see how they disappear.

For this recipe I dip pieces of tofu in the batter accompanied by a piquant sweet and sour sauce which compliments the more bland taste of tofu. As it is best to let the batter stand for ½ hour make it first and set aside while you prepare the sauce.

450 g/1 lb firm tofu cut into 2.5 cm/1 in cubes
shoyu (naturally fermented soya sauce) for coating

soya oil for deep frying
small shallow bowl of wholemeal flour

1. In a shallow bowl sprinkle shoyu over the cubes of tofu and let stand to marinate.

For the Batter

85 g/3 oz gram flour (chick pea flour)	*just under 1 level teaspoon baking powder*
45 g/1 ½ oz soya flour	*just under 1 level teaspoon sea salt*
45 g/1 ½ oz brown rice flour	*about 27 ml/9 fl oz cold water*

1. Sieve the flours into a mixing bowl with the baking powder and sea salt. Gradually add the water to form a smooth, light creamy batter. Cover and let stand for ½ hour, while you prepare the sauce.

For the Sauce

Using sesame oil gives this sauce a wonderful flavour but it is expensive. Sunflower oil is a good cheaper substitute. Also you can use slivers of turnip instead of bamboo shoots if these are difficult to find or too expensive. Five spice is a common oriental mixture of star anise, fennel, cinnamon, clove and pepper and gives the sauce an authentic Eastern flavour. Allspice is a reasonable substitute.

3 tablespoons sesame seed or sunflower seed oil	*ginger*
	½ level teaspoon five spice or allspice
1 medium sized onion, peeled and finely chopped	*115 g/4 oz fresh pineapple, finely chopped*
2 cloves garlic, crushed	
1 medium sized carrot, scraped and thinly sliced in slanting ovals	*1 ½ tablespoons clear honey*
	3 tablespoons cider vinegar
1 small tin bamboo shoots, well drained and sliced or *1 small turnip, thinly sliced*	*2 tablespoons shoyu (naturally fermented soya sauce)*
	2 tablespoons tomato purée
1 small green pepper, cut in thinnish rings, then quartered	*1 tablespoon arrowroot*
	280 ml/10 fl oz water
1 level teaspoon freshly grated root	

1. Stir-fry quickly in hot oil the onions, garlic, carrots, and bamboo shoots or turnip for 3 minutes only.
2. Add the peppers and continue to stir-fry for 2 more minutes.
3. Stir in the grated ginger, five spice or allspice and chopped pineapple. Set aside while you mix all the other ingredients in a medium sized bowl, gradually adding the water as you would to make a batter.
4. Pour this over the vegetables.
5. Return to gentle heat and let cook until the mixture thickens slightly, stirring all the time.
6. Set aside to reheat when the tofu tempura is ready.
7. Now return to the tofu and heat soya oil in a deep frying pan.
8. Fork each piece of tofu, letting excess shoyu drip back into the dish. Roll each in wholemeal flour, dip into the batter by placing each piece again on a fork letting excess batter drip back into the bowl. Deep fry until golden brown.
9. Drain on absorbent kitchen paper and place in a serving dish, pouring the hot sweet and sour sauce over the top.

Serve with plain boiled brown rice, see pages 25–6. I use Surinam long grain rice for Eastern type dishes as it is lighter in texture and takes only 25 minutes to cook.

Oriental Spiced Vegetables with Tofu
Serves 4

This recipe is based on one which I concocted to accompany steamed fish such as salmon trout or unsmoked haddock several years ago. It is equally tasty with pan-fried tofu steaks. You can use 2 tablespoons lemon juice plus curl of lemon peel instead of the tamarind. Serve with Surinam brown rice.

450 g/l lb firm tofu, cut into
   2 cm/¾ in thick slices
shoyu (naturally fermented soya

sauce) for coating
soya oil for quick sautéing

For the Spiced Vegetable Sauce

45 g/1½ oz piece of tamarind (or
   lemon juice and peel)
½ cup boiling water to soak
   tamarind
285 ml/½ pint boiling water
1 bay leaf
1 cinnamon stick
170 g/6 oz peeled onion, cut into
   thin rings
170 g/6 oz green pepper, coarsely
   chopped
115 g/4 oz small button

mushrooms, sliced
2 tablespoons sesame oil or
   sunflower oil
1 slightly rounded tablespoon 100
   per cent wholemeal flour, plain
1 teaspoon methi (fenugreek leaf)
1 rounded teaspoon medium curry
   powder
340 g/12 oz ripe tomatoes,
   skinned and chopped, or canned
   tomatoes
sea salt, to taste

1. Soak the tamarind in ½ cup of boiling water for 10 minutes.
2. Place slices of tofu in a wide shallow bowl and sprinkle with shoyu. Leave to marinate while you prepare the sauce.
3. Press the tamarind through a sieve and the resulting juice will look like a deep brown thickish syrup. Throw hard tamarind pips away.
4. Place boiling water in a medium sized heavy-based saucepan.
5. Add salt, tamarind syrup, bay leaf, cinnamon stick, onion rings, chopped pepper and mushrooms. Bring back to boil and simmer gently with lid on for 5 minutes only. Remove from heat.
6. Heat oil in a pan, stir in the flour, methi and curry powder and cook on low heat for 2 minutes only. Take off heat.
7. Drain vegetables, place stock water in a jug, remove the bay leaf and cinnamon stick and place vegetables in a casserole dish.
8. Stir the hot stock gradually into the flour mixture until a smooth sauce is achieved.

9. Add the chopped tomatoes and cook for 3 minutes more stirring well in.
10. Now sieve this mixture, pressing well with a wooden spoon to get as much through as possible.
11. The sauce will be a rich, warm brown colour and of a medium batter consistency.
12. Take out one cup of sauce and pour the rest over the vegetables in the casserole. Cover the dish and place on the bottom shelf in the oven on lowest heat to keep warm.
13. Now cook the rice using 340 g/12 oz Surinam (see pages 25–6 for directions on how to cook brown rice), but only simmer for 25 minutes as Surinam is much thinner and lighter in texture than Italian brown rice.
14. While rice is cooking, fry the tofu. Heat 6 tablespoons soya oil in a large frying pan.
15. Using a palette knife lift the slices of tofu into the hot oil and fry quickly on both sides until golden brown.
16. Drain on kitchen paper and put on a separate dish in the oven with the casserole.
17. When rice is ready all the water should have been absorbed. If not, drain off excess and put the rice into a warm serving bowl.
18. When ready to serve, heat the reserved cup of sauce on low heat. Take out casserole and spoon the mixture onto a large, shallow warm serving dish. Arrange the slices of tofu on top then pour the remaining sauce over each slice.

Tofu Burgers
Serves 4

In the list of ingredients you will see bulgur wheat. This is a whole wheat product, highly nutritious, simple to prepare and full of flavour. It is usually sold par-boiled which cuts down the cooking time enormously. The structure of the seed is such that the wheatgerm and bran (fibre) are retained even when steel milled. To make a lovely tabbouleh (Lebanese salad) all you do is soak the bulgur in boiling water for 20 minutes as in this recipe, chop fresh salad vegetables such as tomatoes, spring onions, cucumber etc, add a few sprigs of chopped fresh mint, pour over an olive oil and lemon dressing with garlic, and leave overnight in the fridge to absorb all the flavours. Bulgur is also very good in nut roast instead of breadcrumbs. Use half the amount of dry weight bulgur to nuts.

115 g/4 oz bulgur wheat
2 tablespoons shoyu (naturally fermented soya sauce)
225 g/8 oz firm tofu
2 tablespoons fresh chopped parsley
1 onion, approximately 140 g/5 oz, very finely chopped
1 tablespoon sunflower oil
2 tablespoons green pepper, very finely chopped
freshly ground black pepper
1 level tablespoon arrowroot or 1 medium sized egg
soya oil for frying

1. Put bulgur in a small mixing bowl and stir in the shoyu.
2. Add enough boiling water to just cover by 6 mm/¼ in; cover and let stand for 20 minutes.
3. Sweat the onion in the oil for 5 minutes with lid on until soft.
4. Stir into the bulgur mixture with all the other ingredients. Taste and add more shoyu if necessary.
5. Mould well together with hands and fry in hot oil for 3 minutes on each side until golden.
6. Drain well on kitchen paper and serve hot with a tomato sauce and steamed green vegetables, or cold with salad.

Children like these in baps smeared with tomato sauce for a light lunch. Give them an apple afterwards and they will have had a pretty wholesome mid-day meal.

Pizza Tofu Style
Makes 2 pizzas

I love pizza with dairy cheese such as thinly sliced Mozzarella or, for children, grated farmhouse Cheddar cheese. I also like using tofu as an alternative and for those on a low fat diet it is a must. You can use any bread dough as a base for pizza (preferably wholemeal). When making bread break off a 340-345 g/14 oz piece of the dough, roll it out in bran after the first rising and freeze at this stage if you are not ready to make a pizza. It will only take 1 hour to defrost on the tray. It is then ready to prebake if you wish and fill with the sauce of your choice. You can prebake pizza dough as directed in the method but it is not essential. But it does firm the base and avoid any sogginess.

2 teaspoons dried yeast
285 ml/½ pint warm water
½ teaspoon Barbados sugar
2 tablespoons olive oil
1 teaspoon malt extract

450 g/1 lb wholemeal flour
2 tablespoons sesame seeds
just under 1 level teaspoon sea salt
bran for rolling out the dough

1. Dissolve the yeast in the warm water and stir in the sugar. Let stand to froth in a warm place for about 7 minutes.
2. Warm the olive oil by pouring into a hot cup and stir in the malt extract.
3. Mix flour, seeds and salt together.
4. When yeast liquid is ready, make a well in the flour and pour this into the centre with the olive oil and malt.
5. Form into a dough and knead with floured hands for 7 minutes. Place in an oiled polythene bag and leave to rise until it has doubled in size: approximately 40 minutes to 1 hour. Now prepare the sauce.

For the Sauce and Topping

2 tablespoons olive oil

1 large onion (about 225 g/8 oz when peeled), chopped

2 large cloves of garlic, crushed

794 g/1 lb 12 oz can tomatoes; drain off 225 ml/8 fl oz of juice (reserve for stock or soups), and chop tomatoes

2 generous tablespoons tomato purée

1 teaspoon basil

1 teaspoon oregano

2 bay leaves

1 level teaspoon herb or sea salt

freshly ground black pepper to taste

2 tablespoons olive oil

1 large green pepper or ½ red and ½ green, deseeded and chopped

115 g/4 oz button mushrooms, sliced

2 medium sized courgettes, cut into thin 2.5 cm/1 in long sticks

good pinch herb or sea salt

1 tablespoon lemon juice

450 g/1 lb firm tofu cut in thin slices

55 g/2 oz pumpkin seeds

black olives (stoned), to decorate

little oregano

pinch herb salt

1. Heat oil in a heavy-based saucepan. Sauté onion and garlic for 6 minutes, until tender.
2. Add chopped tomatoes, (less 225 ml/8 fl oz liquid), tomato purée, basil, oregano, bay leaves, herb or sea salt and freshly ground black pepper.
3. Bring to boil and simmer for 30 minutes with lid slightly off so that the mixture evaporates a little while cooking.
4. Meanwhile, sauté the green pepper, mushrooms and courgettes in the oil plus a good pinch of herb or sea salt and a little black pepper if you wish, for 4 minutes only.
5. Stir in the lemon juice. Leave to one side.
6. Preheat oven to 200°C/400°F/Gas 6.
7. When dough has risen, knock back and knead for 2 minutes. Break in two pieces and make a ball of each. Sprinkle the work surface with bran and roll each ball out to fit two 30 cm/12 in well oiled pizza trays. Pinch a lip around the edge to contain the sauce then brush with beaten egg.

8. Prebake in the centre of the oven for 7 minutes and set aside to cool slightly.
9. Ladle equal amounts of the tomato mixture on to the pizza crusts.
10. Spoon on the sautéed peppers, mushrooms and courgettes and spread equal amounts of the tofu slices on top with equal portions of pumpkin seeds, olives, a little oregano and a pinch of herb salt.
11. Bake pizzas on two shelves for 15 minutes, changing the trays round after 8 minutes. If a browner top is required then grill for a few minutes. Let stand for at least 5 minutes before cutting. Serve with a fresh salad.

If you wish to freeze one pizza then bake it for 10 minutes only. Let it get cold and then freeze. Defrost for 1½ hours. Bake it for 10 minutes once defrosted.

Leek and Tofu Quiche
Serves 6

In this recipe you can use either soya milk yoghurt or goat's milk yoghurt (see pages 18–19 and 96). The amounts given fill a 41 cm/9½ in flan case. When making wholemeal pastry I use a creaming and light kneading method to release the gluten, which lightens the pastry dough considerably.

115 g/4 oz polyunsaturated
  margarine
3 tablespoons cold water

225 g/8 oz wholemeal flour, plain
pinch sea salt (optional)

1. Cream margarine, water and 2 tablespoons of the flour in a mixing bowl for one minute.
2. Gradually add the rest of the flour to form a smooth dough. Knead with floured hands on a formica or sealed surface for 2 minutes and then chill for 20 minutes in the fridge or 5

minutes in the freezer. Preheat oven to 190°C/375°F/
Gas 5.
3. Roll out dough on floured surface.
4. Using a palette knife curve an edge on to the rolling pin and
lift the pastry on to the well-oiled quiche case.
5. Trim the edge with a sharp knife, prick the base and bake
blind in centre of the oven for 10 minutes only. Let cool.

For the Filling

2 tablespoons sunflower oil	*225 g/8 oz firm tofu*
225 g/8 oz leeks (weight when washed and trimmed) cut into thin rings	*a little sea salt to taste*
	freshly ground black pepper to taste
3 eggs	*¼ teaspoon dry mustard powder*
140 ml/5 fl oz natural yoghurt, either soya, goat's or cow's	*¼ teaspoon ground mace*
	1 level teaspoon tarragon, plus extra for sprinkling

1. Heat oil in a pan and sauté the sliced leeks for 10 minutes
with the lid on. Set aside to cool.
2. Beat eggs in a mixing bowl, add the natural yoghurt and
whisk in.
3. Crumble the tofu and whisk into the egg mixture.
4. Season with salt and pepper and add the mustard, mace and
tarragon. (A liquidiser or food processor does this in
seconds.)
5. When quiche case is cool, spread the base with the sautéed
leeks, then pour over the tofu mixture. Sprinkle a little more
tarragon on top and bake at 190°C/375°F/Gas 5 for 35
minutes.

Asparagus Quiche with Tofu

The mild taste of tofu does not overpower the delicate flavour of
asparagus. Both seem to complement each other.

Follow the recipe for leek quiche but substitute 285 g/10 oz asparagus for the leeks, add 1 medium sized onion, very finely chopped and sautéed, and 1 tablespoon lemon juice to the tofu mixture. Cut off woody stems from asparagus, steam for 20 minutes. Cut off tips and set aside. Cut the stems into small pieces and sprinkle on the precooked base with the sautéed onion. Pour over the tofu mixture. Dot the top with asparagus tips and a sprinkling of tarragon. Bake in the same way as for Leek and Tofu Quiche.

Mushroom, Courgette and Red Pepper Quiche with Tofu

Again using the same recipe as for Leek and Tofu Quiche, substitute 55 g/2 oz button mushrooms, sliced, 2 medium courgettes cut in thin rings, ¼ red pepper chopped, 1 clove garlic and 1 small onion cut in thin rings for the leeks. Stir-fry this vegetable mixture in a little olive oil. Sprinkle with a teaspoon of shoyu (naturally fermented soya sauce), a little freshly ground black pepper and 1 teaspoon lemon juice. Place on the precooked base, pour over the tofu mixture and use oregano or basil instead of tarragon as a herb.

Tofu Mayonnaise

A liquidiser or food processor is ideal for making mayonnaise but you can use a hand whisk.

225 g/8 oz tofu
3 tablespoons soya milk or goat's milk
3 tablespoons lemon juice
1 very level teaspoon sea salt
½ teaspoon dry mustard powder
freshly ground black pepper
4 tablespoons sunflower oil

Blend all ingredients except the oil until smooth. With motor on high speed trickle in the oil until well mixed.

Horseradish Dressing

1 level teaspoon horseradish powder

Use same ingredients as for Tofu Mayonnaise, but halve the quantity and add the horseradish powder.

'In the Pink' Mayonnaise

Use same ingredients as for Tofu Mayonnaise, but halve the quantity and add:

1 clove garlic, peeled and crushed   *finely chopped*
1 small red pepper, deseeded and   *1 level tablespoon capers*

Blend all ingredients together until smooth and pink. Great for potato salad.

Tofu Apple Mint Dressing

Some apples such as Granny Smiths have a thick skin and do not purée as well as the Golden Delicious variety. I find that when puréed in a blender you cannot feel the texture of the skin. Whichever apples you use purée them with skins on and sieve pressing as much through the mesh as possible after processing.

2 eating apples   *1 very level teaspoon sea salt*
1 clove garlic   *freshly ground black pepper*
3 tablespoons lemon juice   *2 tablespoons sunflower oil*
1 teaspoon clear honey   *(optional, but makes a smoother*
1 tablespoon chopped mint leaves   *dressing)*
225 g/8 oz tofu

1. Core the apples and chop roughly. Purée in a blender with the garlic, lemon juice, honey and mint.
2. Break up tofu and put in blender with the apple mixture plus the salt and black pepper. Blend until smooth, then gradually pour in the oil with motor still on.

Tofu and Avocado Dressing

115 g/4 oz tofu, broken into pieces
1 medium sized avocado, roughly chopped
3 tablespoons olive or sunflower oil
2 tablespoons lemon juice
¼ teaspoon mustard powder
¼ teaspoon freshly ground black pepper
½ very level teaspoon sea salt
½ teaspoon clear honey
1 small clove garlic, crushed

Blend all the ingredients in a liquidiser or food processor until smooth and pale green in colour. This looks and tastes beautiful on a mixed green salad, crisp lettuce, watercress, cucumber, parsley etc. Just trickle the dressing over the arranged salad and fork in when ready to serve.

Tofu Dip Delight

This is very good for a buffet party. Fresh herbs are best. In case they are not available I have given the quantities for dried, but I do not like using dried parsley or mint in this recipe. In the recipe I have put cold pressed sunflower or safflower oil. These oils have the most delicious flavour and are traditionally pressed from the seed without heat and retain their nutritional value. They are high in polyunsaturates and linoleic acid which seem to play an important part in controlling cholesterol levels in the blood. Safflower oil has the highest linoleic content. You can use soya milk yoghurt cheese instead of tofu (see pages 19–20 for recipe), but use 1 tablespoon less lemon juice.

450 g/1 lb tofu

4 tablespoons cold pressed safflower or sunflower oil

3 tablespoons lemon juice or half and half wine vinegar and lemon juice

1 teaspoon clear honey

2 tablespoons fresh parsley, very finely chopped

1 tablespoon fresh mint, very finely chopped

1 ½ tablespoons fresh finely chopped marjoram, basil or

oregano, or a little of all three (If using dried, then ½ level teaspoon of all three)

1 medium sized onion, very finely chopped

1 medium sized red pepper, very finely chopped

16 cm/6 in piece of cucumber, diced

1 tablespoon capers

sea salt and freshly ground black pepper to taste

1. Blend tofu, oil, lemon juice and honey in a liquidiser or food processor until smooth.
2. Stir in all the other ingredients, making sure that the vegetables are very finely chopped. Add the salt and pepper last.

You will end up with a lively, crunchy dip. Chill before serving.

This is really good stuffed in pitta bread, in sandwiches, or dolloped in crisp lettuce leaves on a platter for a buffet party. Alternatively just use it as a dip scooped up with whole grain corn crisps (buy these at a health store), or on finger croûtons (garlic-buttered, oven-toasted fingers of wholemeal bread).

Yes, you can make the most mouthwatering sweet dishes such as cheesecake and ice cream without using thick cream and white sugar. Here is a selection of those treats that most of us seem to need either between meals or as dessert.

Lemon and Tofu Cheesecake

This recipe fills a 23 cm/9 in loose-bottomed tin. I use fructose natural·fruit sugar. It looks like castor sugar but is absorbed more slowly from the intestinal tract than sucrose (ordinary sugar) and does not cause the blood sugar levels to rise so sharply. But all sugars, including honey and fruit concentrates such as apple juice concentrate, are equally bad for your teeth and should be eaten as an occasional treat.

You can use soya yoghurt cheese, or goat's milk yoghurt cheese (see pages 19–20 and 97).

170 g/6 oz wholemeal digestive biscuits	*½ teaspoon ground cinnamon*
55 g/2 oz sesame seeds	*85 g/3 oz polyunsaturated margarine, melted*

1. Preheat oven to 150°C/300°F/Gas 2.
2. Break biscuits up and mash with a potato masher, or use your hands, to make into tiny crumbs.
3. Fork in the sesame seeds, cinnamon and the melted margarine.
4. Press evenly into the well oiled tin and bake in the preheated oven for 5 minutes only. Allow to get completely cold.

For the Filling and Topping

284 g/10 oz firm tofu	*few drops of vanilla essence*
good pinch sea salt (optional)	*2 tablespoons yoghurt cheese*
225 g/8 oz yoghurt cheese (use either soya, goat's or cow's)	*any soft fruit such as strawberries, raspberries, stoned morello*
115 g/4 oz fructose	*cherries, or thin wedges of*
60 ml/2 fl oz sunflower oil	*apricôts soaked for a few hours*
3 eggs, separated	*in apple juice concentrate and*
2 tablespoons lemon juice	*drained*
finely grated rind of 1 lemon	

Preheat oven to 150°C/300°F/Gas 2 once more.

1. Cream together the tofu, sea salt, if wished, yoghurt cheese and the fructose for 3 minutes.
2. Pour in the oil and blend together.
3. Beat the egg yolks well and add to creamed mixture.
4. Stir in the lemon juice and rind and vanilla.
5. Whisk the egg whites until stiff.
6. Fold into the mixture.
7. Pour into the cold biscuit base and bake for about 1 hour or until filling is firm in the middle.
8. When cool, chill thoroughly.
9. When quite cold spread on the 2 tablespoons of thick creamy yoghurt and dot with the fruit of your choice.

Banana, Orange and Hazelnut Flan

This recipe will fit a 23 cm/9 in flan dish. You can use the biscuit base, see page 41 for recipe, or the sweet short crust pastry I give here. You can use all wholemeal flour and omit the egg yolk substituting it with an extra tablespoon of cold water. But the ingredients given achieve a very light pastry.

1 level dessertspoon fruit sugar (see page 41 for notes on this)
85 g/3 oz polyunsaturated margarine
1 egg yolk and 1 tablespoon cold
water or 2 tablespoons cold water
115 g/4 oz wholemeal flour, plain
55 g/2 oz unbleached white flour
pinch sea salt (optional)

1. Cream the sugar with the margarine until smooth, about 1 minute.
2. Whisk the egg yolk with the cold water until it froths, then add to creamed mixture. Or add only 2 tablespoons cold water.
3. Sieve the flours with salt, if wished, add 2 tablespoons to the creamed mixture at the same time as adding the egg liquid. Blend well together and gradually add the rest of the flour.

4. Form into a dough. Flour hands and knead for 2 minutes.
5. Place in a polythene bag and refrigerate for 30 minutes.
6. Preheat oven to 190°C/375°F/Gas 5.
7. When well chilled roll pastry out on floured surface. Lift onto the rolling pin and place in the well-oiled flan dish.
8. Trim and crimp edges, prick the base and bake blind for 15 to 20 minutes. Do not burn. Cover with greaseproof paper if edges are getting too brown. Allow to get cold.

For the Filling

3 good sized bananas, sliced
115 g/4 oz fruit sugar or clear
  honey
grated rind of 1 orange
1 tablespoon orange juice
1 tablespoon lemon juice

2 drops vanilla essence
140 ml/4 fl oz sunflower oil
¼ teaspoon sea salt
340 g/12 oz firm tofu
55 g/2 oz roughly ground and
  toasted hazelnuts

1. Purée all ingredients except tofu and hazelnuts in a blender or food processor.
2. When smooth break up tofu and gradually blend into the banana mixture.
3. Pour into the cold cooked pastry case or biscuit base and chill for 3 hours.
4. Toast the roughly ground hazelnuts in the oven for 15 minutes at 170°C/325°F/Gas 3. Take care not to burn. When cold sprinkle on the chilled flan.

Note: For another uncooked absolutely delicious filling using a biscuit base turn to pages 109–10 for Chilled Mango Cheese Pie. In this recipe I used goat's milk cheese and yoghurt cheese but you can use tofu and yoghurt cheese. Try it – it's great!

Carob and Pecan Nut Cake

No egg, no sugar, no margarine or butter needed. This makes a very tasty and nutritious cake and is very simple to make. It fits a 23 cm/9 in cake tin, oiled and lined.

170 g/6 oz clear honey
140 ml/¼ pint sunflower oil
340 g/12 oz firm tofu
½ teaspoon sea salt
four drops of vanilla essence
85 g/3 oz pecan nuts, (chop

55 g/2 oz; leave 30 g/1 oz in
halves to decorate)
235 g/9 oz wholemeal flour, self-
raising
55 g/2 oz carob powder
1 very level teaspoon cinnamon

1. Preheat oven to 150°C/300°F/Gas 4.
2. Blend honey, oil, tofu and sea salt and vanilla essence well together.
3. Stir in the chopped pecans.
4. Sift the flour, carob powder and cinnamon, and gradually add it to the tofu mixture.
5. Spoon into the oiled and lined cake tin and dot with the pecan nut halves. Bake for 30 to 35 minutes. Test centre by inserting a sharp knife. If it comes out clean then your cake is done.

Tofu Light Fruit Cake

To fit a 25 cm/10 in round cake tin, oiled and lined.

140 ml/¼ pint sunflower oil
340 g/12 oz firm tofu
½ teaspoon sea salt
170 g/6 oz clear honey
few drops vanilla essence
310 g/10 oz wholemeal self-
raising flour
1 level teaspoon fresh ground
nutmeg

½ teaspoon ground cinnamon
30 g/1 oz blanched almonds and a
few glacé cherry halves to
decorate
55 g/2 oz sultanas
55 g/2 oz raisins
55 g/2 oz pre-soaked dried
apricots, chopped and soaked in
apple juice for 1 hour

1. Preheat oven to 150°C/300°F/Gas 2. Blend oil, tofu, salt, honey and vanilla in a large mixing bowl.
2. Sift flour with spices and gradually add to the tofu mixture, mixing well in.
3. Stir in the ground almonds and the dried fruit, making sure the soaked apricots have all surface moisture removed on absorbent kitchen paper.
4. Spoon into the prepared tin and bake for 40 to 45 minutes. Test centre with a sharp knife; if it comes out clean then the cake is done.

Now I will give you a few recipes for making ice cream with soya milk. For best results use a rich soya milk. Follow the recipe for making soya milk (pages 13–14) but use 850 ml/1½ pints less water. If you have an ice cream maker all the better but if not, follow directions for freezing in the recipe.

Basic Vanilla Soya Ice Cream
Serves 6

115 g/4 oz fruit sugar
650 ml/1¼ pints rich soya milk
8 drops vanilla essence

4 tablespoons cold pressed
   sunflower oil
good pinch sea salt

1. Blend all ingredients in a liquidiser or food processor.
2. Place them in your ice cream maker, then put them into a plastic container with a lid and place in the freezer compartment of your fridge. Leave there until it begins to set. Beat it again and return to the freezer.

Carob and Hazelnut Soya Ice Cream

Add 2 rounded tablespoons sieved carob powder and 55 g/2 oz

roughly chopped toasted and cooled hazelnuts. Blend with other ingredients and freeze as directed.

Strawberry, Raspberry or Blackcurrant Soya Ice Cream

Add 225 g/8 oz strawberries, raspberries or blackcurrants and blend with other ingredients. If you do not want the seeds then press the fruit through a sieve and add the purée to the other ingredients. Freeze as directed.

Soya Yoghurt Ice Cream

This is easily made. Just substitute soya milk yoghurt (see pages 18–19 for recipe) for the rich soya milk in all the soya ice cream recipes.

Finally I will give you a recipe using the pulp (okara) which is left after making soya milk (for notes on okara see page 13). It's a wonderful wholesome breakfast treat and makes delicious flapjacks.

Toasted Okara Granola Breakfast

450 g/1 lb okara
115 g/4 oz hazelnuts
225 g/8 oz porridge oats
3 generous tablespoons malt extra
3 tablespoons clear honey
3 tablespoons sunflower oil

85 g/3 oz sesame seeds
85 g/3 oz sunflower seeds
good pinch sea salt
225 g/8 oz mixed raisins, dried apricots, chopped and dates, chopped

1. Dry okara by spreading it on a baking sheet and baking for 30 minutes, at 150°C/300°F/Gas 2. Do not brown – just let it dry. Stir it occasionally.

2. At the same time toast the hazelnuts on the top shelf until light brown inside for about the same time as it takes to dry the okara.

3. Place the dry okara and all the other ingredients, except the hazelnuts and the dried fruit, into a large heavy-based saucepan. Toast the mixture over a low to medium heat stirring constantly to prevent burning until it is crisp and golden brown.

4. Let it cool and stir in the toasted hazelnuts and the dried fruit.

Store in airtight jars and serve with yoghurt and fresh fruit for a truly healthy start to the day. Makes about 1.1 kg/2½ lb.

Tempeh

Tempeh is a most delicious complete protein food which originates from Indonesia where it has been a staple food for hundreds of years. It is made with a natural culture similar to those used in cheese and yoghurt making. The partially cooked and split beans are mixed with the starter (culture) which ferments slowly over approximately 24 to 30 hours. During the fermentation period the protein is broken down, making the tempeh an easily digestible food. When fermented, the soya beans are of a higher nutritional value, containing vitamin B12 and more B6 Riboflavin and Niacin than when unfermented. The culture used is Rhizopus oligosporus which can be obtained by mail order (for address see page 140).

Tempeh, as well as being a high protein, easily digestible food, is low in fat, has no cholesterol and is rich in iron. It has a chicken-like flavour, smells like fresh mushrooms and is good for barbecuing, baking in casseroles, adding to vegetable sauces or simply deep fried. 225 g/8 oz of tempeh will be sufficient for four servings; 55 g/2 oz will provide approximately 10 g/½ oz of complete protein which is one third of the adult recommended daily requirement. By combining tempeh with grains and fresh vegetables, cheese or cheese sauces as is usual when eating tempeh, the amount of complete protein made available to the body is increased by approximately one third. You can also eat tempeh with meat using half meat and half tempeh.

The process of making tempeh is quite a lengthy one but extremely exciting and worth doing in big batches which can be frozen. To freeze it, it is best to first steam pieces of freshly made tempeh for 5 minutes. Let cool and place portions in polythene bags. Refrigerated it will last for 4 days but do not stack pieces of uncooked tempeh on top of each other as the culture continues to grow and produces heat which ruins the tempeh. Once you make tempeh you will want, I'm sure, to prepare and eat this food often. Children seem to like the savoury taste which is a boon as many young children have rather temperamental eating habits.

How to Make Tempeh

You will need a large wire cooling rack and polythene bags which you perforate with a needle so that the upper and underside holes are approximately 2.5 cm/1 in apart.

450 g/1 lb dry weight soya beans   *1 ½ tablespoons cider vinegar*
1.7 litres/3 pints water for   *1 teaspoon tempeh starter*
  soaking beans

1. Bring beans just to boiling point in the water. Remove from heat, cover and let stand at room temperature for 12 hours.
2. Pour off the soaking water and rub the beans vigorously to loosen the hulls.
3. Pour on fresh water, stir and skim off as many of the hulls as you can. Pour off the water and repeat this process several times until the hulls have been removed. (A few left will not matter but the tempeh has a better flavour without them.)
4. After rubbing, the beans will be split in half and ready to cook.
5. Pour on 1.7 litres/3 pints of hot water and the vinegar. Bring to boil and cook uncovered for 45 minutes making sure that the water is gently bubbling all the time.
6. Now drain the beans and towel dry, massaging excess moisture away. (If the beans are wet you are likely to fail in making edible tempeh.)
7. When cool and easy to touch, which takes about 7 minutes, place in a mixing bowl, stir in the culture and mix well for 1 ½ to 2 hours.
8. Spoon the bean mixture into the perforated plastic bags until half full. Seal the open ends and flatten mixture to 1.5 cm/½ in thickness.
9. Put flattened bags on a cooling rack so that air can

    circulate all around because the growing culture needs oxygen.

10. Put the rack in a warm place (about 30°-32°C/86°-90°F is ideal) to incubate for 20 to 30 hours. A south-facing sunny window, a warm shelf area in the kitchen or in an airing cupboard which has a light are ideal places for the incubation period but check the temperature occasionally as the tempeh produces its own heat and many failures occur through overheating.

11. A white mould begins to appear after the first 12 hours. This white mould looks like frost after 20 to 25 hours.

12. At the slightest tinge of grey your tempeh is done.

For storing and freezing see page 48 and follow directions carefully.

    Perfect Tempeh is when the beans are tightly bound by a whitish grey mycelium or mould which spreads branch-like throughout the cake, smells fresh and faintly of fresh mushrooms and does not crumble when sliced.

    Imperfect Tempeh is characterised by the mycelium being pure white and not filling the areas between the beans snugly. This can be caused by either too short an incubation period, or an uneven distribution of the starter which means there is an uneven heat during fermentation. This tempeh crumbles when cut, has a harder texture and lacks flavour when cooked.

    Over-ripe Tempeh is when the mould is grey/black. This is due to sporulation. The tempeh is still safe to eat but it is stronger in taste and smells slightly of ammonia.

    Ruined Tempeh smells very strongly of ammonia or other unpleasant odours and can have a slimy surface. This should be discarded. If the mould is any colour other than white, grey or grey/black it is unsafe to eat (eg red, green or yellow).

    In America it is possible to buy tempeh in health stores and some supermarkets and it looks as if we too will be able to buy this wonderful food in our own shops in the near future.

Recipes Using Tempeh

Tempeh can be served in a variety of exciting ways. Its delicate flavour enhances as well as absorbs the flavours of other foods including herbs and spices. It is also quick to prepare almost instant meals once you have a stock in the freezer. I hope tempeh will be available in vacuum or frozen packs in our shops in the near future for those who want to eat tempeh but are perhaps too busy to make it at home.

Now for some recipes which I hope will be delicious as well as nourishing. I will start with simple everyday fare and then give you some gourmet recipes. When you have tried out my recipes you could experiment with traditional recipes for sauces which go with left-over poultry or veal and you will find that the ingredients complement tempeh as they do meat.

Tempeh Tabbouleh (Bulgur Wheat Salad)
Serves 4

Delicious served with thick natural yoghurt.

225 g/8 oz bulgur wheat
2 tablespoons shoyu
225 g/8 oz tempeh
4 tablespoons olive oil or cold pressed sunflower oil
3 tablespoons lemon juice
2 large cloves garlic, crushed
1 level teaspoon ground coriander seeds
½ level teaspoon ground cumin
½ level teaspoon freshly ground black pepper

¼ teaspoon clear honey
1 bunch spring onions, finely chopped or small onion, very finely chopped
30 g/1 oz parsley, finely chopped
15 g/½ oz fresh mint, finely chopped
6 firm tomatoes, cut in small wedges
55 g/2 oz pine nuts (optional but delicious)
1 bunch watercress to garnish

1. Soak the bulgur in enough boiling water to cover by

2 cm/¾ in. Stir in 1 tablespoon of the shoyu. Cover and leave to stand for 20 to 30 minutes.

2. Meanwhile, steam tempeh for 10 minutes, take out and cut into small pieces.

3. Place oil, lemon juice, garlic, coriander, cumin, black pepper, honey and the rest of the shoyu in a screw-top jar. Shake well.

4. Put cut steamed tempeh in a shallow dish. Pour over the dressing and let marinate until the bulgur is ready.

5. Stir spring onions, parsley, mint and tomatoes into the bulgur.

6. Stir in the marinated tempeh dressing and half the pine nuts, if used.

Garnish with the remaining pine nuts and sprigs of watercress.
   This salad improves with keeping for 24 hours but garnish with the watercress just before serving.

Winter Salad with Tempeh
Serves 4

This salad – served with wholemeal High Protein Loaf (see pages 135–6) – will provide a very non-fattening, wholesome lunch or late supper-time filler. I advise using cold pressed oils such as sunflower, safflower, sesame or olive oil (see notes on fats, page 39) in salad dressings or stir-fried dishes.

285 ml/½ pint stock or water to which you have added ¾ vegetable stock cube
2 medium sized carrots, scraped and cut into small cubes
2 medium sized potatoes, scrubbed and cut into small cubes
225 g/8 oz tempeh, cut in small

chunks
115 g/4 oz frozen peas
2 tender sticks celery, finely chopped
1 small onion, finely chopped
15 cm/6 in piece of cucumber, cut into small chunks
1 tablespoon fresh chopped parsley, plus a little for garnishing

140 ml/¼ pint lemon mayonnaise   1 tablespoon capers or home-made
2 tablespoons natural yoghurt   chutney

1. Bring stock to boil and simmer carrots and potatoes in this
   for 5 minutes until just tender but still firm.
2. Drain and reserve liquid. Place carrots and potatoes in a
   serving bowl.
3. Bring stock to boil and simmer tempeh for 10 minutes; add
   the peas and continue to cook for 3 to 4 more minutes only.
4. Drain and add tempeh and peas to carrots and potatoes.
5. Stir in the celery, onion, cucumber, parsley, mayonnaise,
   yoghurt and capers or chutney.

Garnish with a little more parsley. Eat either warm or cold and
serve with High Protein Loaf (see pages 135–6 for recipe) for a
wholesome lunch or supper-time filler.

Pasta and Tempeh Niçoise
Serves 4

240 ml/8 fl oz stock or water to   ½ medium sized cucumber, cut
   which you have added   into small chunks
   ¾ vegetable stock cube   1 very small onion, very finely
225 g/8 oz tempeh   chopped
115 g/4 oz pasta twists (cooked,   170 g/6 oz cooked French beans,
   drained and cooled). (You can   cut into 2.5 cm/1 in pieces
   cook pasta in the tempeh stock   55 g/2 oz black olives, stoned and
   water.)   chopped
225 g/8 oz firm tomatoes,   1 tablespoon freshly chopped
   chopped   parsley

Dressing
3 tablespoons cold pressed olive oil   ½ level teaspoon sea salt
1 tablespoon lemon juice   ¼ teaspoon freshly ground black
1 teaspoon finely grated lemon peel   pepper
1 level teaspoon basil   1 clove garlic, crushed

1. Bring stock to boil in a shallow pan. Simmer tempeh for 3 minutes with lid on. Turn tempeh and simmer for 5 more minutes. Remove tempeh from water with a slotted spoon or fish slice and let cool.
2. Cut tempeh into 6 mm/¼ in cubes.
3. Combine tempeh with cooked pasta twists, tomatoes, cucumber, onion, French beans, olives and parsley.
4. Shake the dressing ingredients in a screw-top jar and pour over the salad.

Let stand for half an hour to let the flavours blend.

Tempeh Nutty Pâté

This rich pâté has a smooth texture and will keep for one week in the fridge. It is just perfect for a buffet party. You will need a food processor or a blender.

55 g/2 oz whole almonds
55 g/2 oz hazelnuts
4 tablespoons cold pressed sunflower oil
1 clove garlic, crushed
1 small onion, finely chopped
225 g/½ lb sliced button mushrooms
225 g/8 oz tempeh cut into

2.5 cm/1 in pieces
good pinch sea salt
1 teaspoon sweet mixed herbs
1 tablespoon shoyu (or more, to your taste)
55 g/2 oz pistachio nuts
3 tablespoons sunflower oil (to grind nuts with)
freshly ground black pepper to taste

1. Toast the almonds and hazelnuts in the oven at 170°C/325°F/Gas 3 for approximately 20 minutes until lightly browned.
2. Heat the 4 tablespoons of sunflower oil in a pan and sauté garlic, onion and mushrooms until soft – about 5 minutes.
3. Add the tempeh, pinch sea salt and mixed herbs and cook gently for 10 minutes with lid off to let the liquid evaporate.

4. Stir in the shoyu.
5. Grind toasted almonds, hazelnuts and pistachio nuts in a blender or food processor until very fine.
6. Add 3 tablespoons of sunflower oil and blend well together.
7. Gradually add the sautéed tempeh mixture and blend until mixture is smooth and thick.
8. Scoop out, place in a serving dish and sprinkle freshly ground black pepper over the top.

Andalusian Salad Soup with Tempeh
Serves 6

This chilled gazpacho can be served as a starter for 6 or as a substantial main meal for 4. It delights the eye accompanied by a variety of colourful, crisp, fresh garnishes. This is a must for hot summer days.

4 thick slices of wholemeal bread
3 tablespoons olive oil
1 large Spanish onion, finely chopped
2 cloves garlic, crushed
1 small red pepper, chopped
2 medium courgettes, chopped
450 g/1 lb ripe tomatoes, skinned
and chopped
2 tablespoons tomato purée
285 ml/½ pint water
3 tablespoons mayonnaise
425 ml/¾ pint approximately iced water
sea salt and freshly ground black pepper

1. Crumble the bread into very fine crumbs and place in a mixing bowl.
2. Heat the oil in a heavy-based saucepan and sauté the onion, garlic, pepper and courgettes for 7 minutes with the lid on. Scoop out and stir into the breadcrumbs.
3. Blend tomatoes, tomato purée and the 285 ml/½ pint water in a liquidiser or food processor and pour over the breadcrumb mixture. Mix well.

4. Now return half the mixture to the liquidiser or food processor and blend until very smooth.
5. Repeat with the other half of the mixture.
6. Pour mixture into the serving bowl, stir in the mayonnaise and enough of the 425 ml/¾ pint iced water to give the consistency of thin batter or single cream.
7. Season with sea salt and freshly ground black pepper.
8. Chill well before serving.

Garnishes

These are arranged in separate bowls and spooned into individual portions of the soup when ready to eat.

I suggest small bowls of thinly sliced onion rings, chopped cucumber, lightly cooked French beans chopped in 2 cm/¾ in pieces, stoned olives and Crispy Fried Tempeh, for which I will now give you the recipe.

Crispy Fried Tempeh
Serves 4

225 g/8 oz tempeh
1 tablespoon shoyu (naturally fermented soya sauce)
1 tablespoon cherry or red grape juice
1 clove garlic, minced
gram flour (chick pea flour) or wholemeal flour for dusting
oil for deep frying

1. Cut tempeh into 2 cm/¾ in cubes. Blend shoyu, juice and garlic together and place in a shallow bowl. Marinate the tempeh in this for 15 minutes or longer, turning occasionally to coat all sides.
2. Roll each cube in the flour and let stand on a clean plate for 5 minutes.
3. Heat oil in a frying pan (not a chipper).
4. Carefully place the floured tempeh pieces into the hot oil. Do not crowd the pan.

5. Fry until golden brown and crisp. Drain on absorbent kitchen paper.

Serve with the other garnishes but do not mix in with soup. Best eaten from side plates.

Indian Mango Curry Soup
Serves 6

This is a wonderful starter which surprises all those who taste it for the first time. Although mangoes are very expensive, a mango gives this soup a very special flavour. Serve hot or chilled.

1.1 litres/2 pints stock or hot water to which you have added 2 vegetable stock cubes

225 g/8 oz tempeh, chopped into small pieces

2 tablespoons sunflower oil

1 large onion, finely chopped

2 medium sized carrots, finely chopped

2 sticks celery, finely chopped

2 tablespoons unbleached white flour

1 very level dessertspoon curry powder

1 tablespoon lemon juice

1 mango, peeled, stoned and chopped

1 teaspoon methi (fenugreek leaf) to garnish

1. Bring stock to boil and cook tempeh, simmering gently for 10 minutes.
2. Heat oil in a pan and sauté the onion, carrots and celery until onion is transparent.
3. Stir in the flour and curry powder and cook gently over moderate heat stirring constantly for 2 minutes.
4. Gradually pour in the hot stock and tempeh, stirring constantly.
5. Bring to boil and simmer gently for 20 minutes. Take off heat. Stir in the lemon juice and mango.

6. Liquidise until smooth.
7. Reheat before serving but do not boil. Garnish with a little methi (fenugreek leaf).

This soup is also delicious served chilled.

Tomato Broth with Tempeh Dumplings
Serves 4

This soup is a meal in itself. Eaten with garlic wholemeal French loaf it will provide four good servings or 6 as a starter.

1 large onion, finely chopped
1 large clove garlic (more if you wish)
3 tablespoons sunflower oil
115 g/4 oz short grain brown rice (dry weight) washed and drained
1 litre/1 ¾ pints hot water
1 vegetable stock cube
1 bay leaf
2 medium sized potatoes, scrubbed and diced

2 medium sized carrots, scrubbed and diced
3 sticks celery, chopped
l level teaspoon sweet basil, dried
½ teaspoon dried tarragon
450 g/1 lb ripe soft tomatoes, skinned
1 tablespoon tomato purée
1 tablespoon shoyu (naturally fermented soya sauce)
freshly ground black pepper

1. Sauté onion and garlic in the oil in a large heavy-based saucepan until soft, about 6 minutes.
2. Stir in the brown rice and fry gently for a few minutes more.
3. Pour in the hot water, stock cube and bay leaf.
4. Bring to boil and simmer with lid on for 20 minutes.
5. Add the potatoes, carrots, celery and herbs and cook for 10 minutes more with lid on.
6. Purée the skinned tomatoes and add these with the tomato purée. Continue to cook for 5 more minutes.
7. Stir in shoyu and freshly ground black pepper. Set aside to reheat when dumplings are ready.

For the Dumplings

225 g/8 oz tempeh, chopped into small pieces

1 egg

140 ml/¼ pint soya milk, goat's milk or cow's milk

¼ teaspoon freshly ground black pepper

¼ teaspoon mustard powder

115 g/4 oz wholemeal flour

1 level teaspoon baking powder

½ teaspoon sea salt or 1 dessert-spoon shoyu (more if you wish)

1 litre/1 ¾ pints stock or hot water to which you have added 2 level teaspoons herb salt

1. Blend the tempeh, egg, milk, pepper and mustard in a food processor or liquidiser until smooth, about 1 minute.
2. Sift flour, baking powder and sea salt or shoyu together and blend with other ingredients. You will end up with a thick batter.
3. In a deep frying pan bring the stock or water to boil and, using a tablespoon, drop four to five spoonfuls of the mixture into the boiling water. Make sure that you give the spoonfuls enough space to expand without touching each other.
4. Cover pan and simmer for 5 minutes, turn the dumplings over and cook for a further 5 minutes with lid off. Keep warm in a large covered dish in the oven. (Note: save the stock water and use for sauces, gravies or soups.)
5. Finally, reheat the tomato broth and gently place the dumplings in. Do not boil but let dumplings absorb the flavour of the broth before serving.

To balance the meal using this recipe as a main course, serve with a fresh salad.

Ratatouille with Tempeh
Serves 4

1 large aubergine
2 good sized courgettes
6 good sized tomatoes
55 g/2 oz small button
    mushrooms
1 medium sized green pepper, de-
    seeded
1 medium sized red pepper
1 large Spanish onion

2 large cloves garlic
5 tablespoons olive oil
225 g/8 oz tempeh cut in
    1.5 cm/½ in pieces
1 bay leaf
1 very level teaspoon sweet basil
sea salt, freshly ground black
    pepper
3 tablespoons red wine (optional)

1. Cut aubergine and courgettes into 1 cm/¼ in thickish slices. Place in a colander with a plate and a weight and leave to stand for 1 hour to press out moisture.
2. Skin and chop the tomatoes, slice the mushrooms and dice the peppers.
3. Coarsely chop onion and sauté with the garlic in the oil over low heat for 5 minutes until soft. Add tempeh and sauté for 3 minutes.
4. Add the peppers and sauté for 5 more minutes.
5. Add the drained aubergines, courgettes, mushrooms, bay leaf and basil and cook gently for 3 minutes.
6. Stir in the tomatoes, season with salt and freshly ground black pepper and let cook for 25 minutes with a lid on. Stir mixture occasionally during cooking time.
7. Stir in the red wine if using and cook for 5 more minutes with lid off.

Serve with wholegrain pasta noodles or bulgur wheat (see page 32 on how to prepare bulgur).

Tempeh Goulash
Serves 4

Very simple and quick to prepare.

1 large onion, finely chopped
1 large clove garlic, crushed
3 tablespoons sunflower oil
1 large green pepper, deseeded and
 chopped
1 bay leaf
1 vegetable stock cube, crumbled
1 slightly rounded tablespoon
 paprika
1 level tablespoon unbleached white

or wholemeal flour
1 rounded tablespoon tomato purée
794 g/1 lb 12oz can tomatoes,
 chopped and puréed in a
 liquidiser
225 g/8 oz tempeh, cut into
 1.25 cm/½ in pieces
1 small carton sour cream or thick
 natural yoghurt

1. Sauté the onion and garlic in the oil for 10 minutes until soft
   and transparent.
2. Add green pepper and continue to sauté for 3 more minutes.
3. Stir in bay leaf, stock cube, paprika and flour and let cook
   very gently for just 1 minute.
4. Add tomato purée and tomatoes. Cook with lid on for 15
   minutes.
5. Add tempeh pieces and continue to cook for 15 minutes
   more. Remove from heat and stir in the sour cream or
   natural yoghurt just before serving with brown rice and a
   simple fresh salad.

Tempeh with Artichokes and Lemon Sauce
Serves 4

This easily prepared dish is perfect served with plain or spinach noodles and garnished with watercress for a special meal.

340 g/12 oz tempeh
wholemeal flour for coating,
*   seasoned with sea salt and*
*   freshly ground black pepper*
3 tablespoons sunflower oil
1 generous tablespoon finely
*   chopped onion*
340 g/12 oz canned artichoke
*   hearts, drained and sliced*

140 ml/¼ pint dry white wine
*   (optional)*
285 ml/½ pint vegetable or
*   chicken stock*
1 tablespoon lemon juice
finely grated rind of 1 lemon
115 g/4 oz sour cream
freshly ground black pepper
watercress, to garnish

1. Cut tempeh in 2.5 × 5 cm/1 × 2 in pieces.
2. Roll in the seasoned flour. Heat oil in a frying pan and sauté the tempeh until lightly browned on both sides.
3. Add onion, artichoke slices, wine, stock, lemon rind and lemon juice. Bring to boil and simmer over low heat with lid on for 20 minutes.
4. Take off heat and stir in the sour cream and freshly ground black pepper. Place in a warm serving dish and garnish with sprigs of watercress.

Tempeh Osso Buco Style
Serves 6

*340 g/12 oz tempeh cut into 6
  portions
1 tablespoon flour for coating, with
  a little sea salt added
3 tablespoons olive or sunflower oil
3 medium sized carrots, very finely
  chopped
2 sticks celery, very finely chopped
1 good sized onion, very finely
  chopped
2 cloves garlic, crushed
200 ml/⅓ pint dry white wine*

*200 ml/⅓ pint hot water, to
  which you have added
  1 vegetable or chicken stock cube
396 g/14 oz can tomatoes,
  liquidised
freshly ground black pepper
½ teaspoon honey (optional)
½ teaspoon dried rosemary or
  1 small sprig of fresh rosemary
3 tablespoons finely chopped parsley
grated rind of 1 large lemon
1 clove garlic, crushed*

1. Coat the tempeh in a little seasoned flour.
2. In a large heavy-based saucepan sauté the floured tempeh in
   hot oil until just light golden on both sides, about 2 minutes.
   Take out and leave to one side.
3. Sauté the very finely chopped carrot, celery and onion and
   garlic for 7 minutes with lid off until lightly browned.
4. Put tempeh back into the pot with vegetables.
5. Pour over the wine, stock and tomatoes.
6. Season with freshly ground black pepper, the honey and
   rosemary. Simmer over low heat with lid on for 25 minutes.
   Uncover and cook gently for 5 more minutes.
7. Mix garnish ingredients together.
8. Using a slotted spoon or fish slice remove tempeh carefully
   and place on a warm serving dish. Pour sauce over this and
   sprinkle on the garnish.

Serve with tagliatelle pasta or boiled rice and a fresh salad for a
truly delightful dinner-party dish.

Tempeh à l'Orange
Serves 4

340 g/12 oz tempeh cut into four portions
juice of 1 orange
1 good pinch sea salt
1 clove garlic, crushed
1 rounded tablespoon gram (chick pea flour) or wholemeal flour
sea salt and freshly ground black pepper

finely grated rind of 1 orange
3 tablespoons sunflower oil
285 ml/½ pint sour cream or just under 285 ml/½ pint natural yoghurt and a generous tablespoon curd or cream cheese
1 tablespoon Grand Marnier (optional)

1. Steam tempeh for 10 minutes. Take out with fish slice.
2. Marinate the tempeh portions in the orange juice, pinch sea salt and the crushed garlic for 20 minutes, turning occasionally to coat all sides.
3. Combine flour, orange rind, a little sea salt and black pepper in a small shallow bowl.
4. Dip the marinated tempeh thoroughly in this coating.
5. Heat oil in frying pan and gently sauté the tempeh until light golden brown on both sides. Take out and place in a warm serving dish.
6. Pour the marinated liquid, plus the sour cream or yoghurt and curd cheese mixture into the pan. Stir well. Season with sea salt and black pepper if wished.
7. Stir in the Grand Marnier just before serving. Finally pour the sauce over the fried tempeh.

This recipe is delicious served with roast or baked jacket potatoes and a lightly steamed green vegetable.

Stuffed Parsley Pancakes with Chilli Tempeh
Makes 10

It is a good idea to make the pancakes in advance as they keep well in the fridge overnight and will freeze well simply stacked on top of each other. It is important to let the batter stand for at least 1 hour, especially when using wholemeal flour. During this period the starchy cells swell, the batter thickens slightly and your pancakes will be lighter.

*115 g/4 oz 100 per cent
    wholemeal flour, plain*
2 eggs
285 ml/½ pint milk

½ teaspoon sea salt
2 tablespoons sunflower oil
55 g/2 oz fresh parsley sprigs
soya oil for frying

For the Filling

225 g/8 oz tempeh
1 large onion, chopped
1 clove garlic, crushed
*3 tablespoons sunflower or olive
    oil*
*1 green eating apple, chopped with
    skin on*
1 good-sized green pepper, chopped
*115 g/¼ lb small button
    mushrooms, thinly sliced*
1 teaspoon oregano
1 bay leaf

*1 level teaspoon cayenne or chilli
    powder*
*396 g/14 oz can tomatoes,
    chopped*
1 tablespoon tomato purée
2 tablespoons apple juice
1 level teaspoon arrowroot
*1 tablespoon shoyu (naturally
    fermented soya sauce)*
2 tablespoons thick natural yoghurt
115 g/4 oz grated Cheddar cheese

1. For the pancakes, if using a liquidiser or food processor simply blend flour, eggs, half the milk and sea salt together until smooth. Gradually add the remaining milk, oil and parsley sprigs and process until smooth and pale green.
2. If mixing by hand using a fork, beat eggs with a little milk and flour. Gradually add more flour and milk alternatively.

Finally stir in the oil and very finely chopped parsley and whisk with a hand whisk for 1 minute.

3. Let batter stand for at least 1 hour.
4. When batter is ready brush a small heavy-based frying pan (a crêpe – pancake – pan is best) with oil. Heat well and place 2 level tablespoons of the batter in the centre, turning down the heat as you do this. Spread batter by tilting the pan, smoothing edges with the back of the spoon until it is thin. Turn up heat and cook for 1 minute. Shake pan, loosen edges with a palette knife and flip pancake over. Cook other side for about 20 to 30 seconds.
5. Stack pancakes on top of each other. They will not stick.

For the Filling

1. Cut tempeh into 1.25 cm/½ in cubes and steam either in a steamer or in a colander over a pan of boiling water for 10 minutes.
2. Sauté onion and garlic in hot oil for 7 minutes. Add tempeh, apple, green pepper, mushrooms, oregano, bay leaf and cayenne or chilli powder. Sauté for 3 more minutes.
3. Stir in the chopped tomatoes.
4. Blend tomato purée and apple juice and stir into the tomato mixture.
5. Mix all well together and simmer gently with lid on for 20 minutes.
6. Blend arrowroot with shoyu and yoghurt and stir in.
7. Fill each pancake with the hot mixture. (It's easier to fill and roll them up in the baking dish.) Sprinkle on the grated cheese and grill under moderate heat until cheese is golden brown.

These pancakes are also delicious stuffed with Bolognese Sauce, see pages 26–7 and with a light cheese sauce poured over the top then baked for 25 minutes.

Curried Tempeh
Serves 6

This recipe has quite a list of ingredients, because I prefer not to use a bought curry powder mixture. Buy small amounts of herbs and spices as they lose their flavour if not used up within a few weeks. Always keep them out of direct sunlight. You will find the flavour of this curry well worth the effort. I have listed the spices separately from the vegetables so that you can have these measured out on a plate before starting the cooking.

Spices

55 g/2 oz tamarind
1 very slightly rounded teaspoon turmeric
1 slightly rounded teaspoon ground cumin
1 slightly rounded teaspoon ground coriander
1 rounded teaspoon methi (fenugreek leaf)
1 level teaspoon chilli powder or

cayenne pepper
3 cardamom, podded and the seeds ground
1 cinnamon stick
¼ teaspoon clove powder
1 rounded teaspoon freshly grated ginger root
1 level teaspoon black mustard seeds

Vegetables

340 g/12 oz tempeh
3 tablespoons sunflower oil
1 large onion, chopped
2 large cloves garlic, crushed
2 medium sized potatoes cut into cubes (leave skins on)
2 tender sticks celery, chopped
½ medium cauliflower, broken into florets

1 large green pepper, chopped
1 small cooking apple, cut into small chunks
4 good sized tomatoes, skinned and chopped
1 tablespoon tomato purée
115 g/4 oz French beans (fresh or frozen), left whole
sea salt to taste

1. Cut tempeh into 1.25 cm/½ in cubes and steam for 10 minutes.

2. Soak the tamarind in 1 teacup boiling water for 20 minutes, then strain through a sieve. You will have a tangy, thickish liquid. Set aside.
3. In a large saucepan heat oil and sauté onion, garlic and cubed potatoes for 10 minutes with lid on.
4. Add tempeh, celery, cauliflower florets, green pepper and cooking apples and continue to cook for 5 more minutes.
5. Now add all the spices and fry for 2 minutes. Take care not to burn the mixture. Stir constantly.
6. Add the chopped tomatoes, tomato purée, tamarind liquid and beans. Stir gently. Bring to boil over medium heat. Turn down to simmer and cook with lid on for 30 to 40 minutes.

Serve with Surinam rice (this is a thin grain similar to Basmati rice, but unlike Basmati it is a whole brown rice which needs only 25 minutes cooking time. See how to cook brown rice on pages 25–6). Yoghurt mixed with cucumber, a little chopped mint and a dash of honey is a perfect accompaniment to any curry dish.

Oriental Tempeh Stew
Serves 4 to 5

340 g/12 oz tempeh
wholemeal flour for coating, seasoned with sea salt and freshly ground black pepper
3 tablespoons sunflower oil
1 good sized carrot
6 large spring onions, including green stems
570 ml/1 pint hot water
1 vegetable or chicken stock cube
1 small clove garlic, crushed

115 g/4 oz button mushrooms
1 level tablespoon tahini (sesame seed paste)
1 level tablespoon tomato purée
2 star anise
½ teaspoon freshly grated ginger root
1 tablespoon shoyu (naturally fermented soya sauce)
2 tablespoons rice wine or sherry
1 level dessertspoon honey

1. Cut tempeh into 2.5 × 5 cm/1 × 2 in strips.
2. Roll these in the seasoned flour.
3. Heat oil in a frying pan and sauté the tempeh until lightly browned on both sides. Take out with a fish slice and drain on kitchen paper.
4. Slice the carrot in very thin slanting ovals.
5. Cut spring onions in thin slanting strips.
6. Bring hot water plus the stock cube to boil and add tempeh, sliced carrot and garlic. Cover and simmer for 5 minutes.
7. Add spring onions and mushrooms, cover and continue to simmer for 5 minutes more.
8. Add all other ingredients. Stir well and cover and let cook for 10 minutes.
9. Take out star anise and serve the stew with plain boiled brown rice and a fresh salad.

Tempeh with Barbecue Sauce
Serves 5

3 tablespoons sunflower oil
1 large onion, finely chopped
2 large cloves garlic, crushed
1 medium green pepper, deseeded and chopped
2 tablespoons fresh chopped parsley
1 heaped teaspoon basil
1 bay leaf
794 g/1 lb 12 oz can tomatoes (less 240 ml/8 fl oz juice)
3 tablespoons tomato purée
1 tablespoon honey or slightly less of molasses
1 level teaspoon cayenne pepper
1 rounded teaspoon paprika
1 level teaspoon mustard powder
4 tablespoons lemon juice or 3 tablespoons cider or raspberry vinegar
1 tablespoon shoyu (naturally fermented soya sauce)
450 g/1 lb tempeh

1. For the sauce: heat oil in a large heavy-based saucepan and sauté onion and garlic for 10 minutes until transparent.
2. Add green pepper and paprika and continue to fry for 3 minutes more.

3. Stir in the parsley, basil, bay leaf, tomatoes, (less the tomato juice stated – this can be used in soups) tomato purée, honey or molasses, cayenne pepper and mustard powder. Bring to boil on moderate heat, stirring constantly. Turn down to simmer and simmer gently for 45 minutes with lid on.

4. Stir in the lemon juice or vinegar and the shoyu. Taste and add more shoyu if needed.

5. Take out bay leaf and liquidise until you get a fine but still slightly rough texture.

6. While sauce is cooking, cut tempeh into 2 cm/¾ in wide strips. Sauté in a little oil over low heat until just lightly browned.

7. Spread a thin layer of barbecue sauce on the bottom of a large baking dish. Place the strips of sautéed tempeh on top and then spoon a generous amount of barbecue sauce over the tempeh. Let this stand for 30 minutes to let the tempeh absorb the flavour of the sauce.

8. Bake at 180°C/350°F/Gas 4 for approximately 15 minutes until the mixture bubbles.

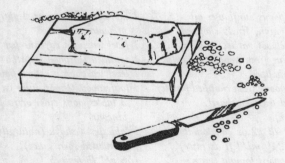

The piquant, tasty sauce will keep in the fridge for 10 days and freezes well. The tempeh can either be baked in the oven with the sauce or basted with the sauce as you grill it over charcoal. This recipe is delicious served hot with rice as a main meal, or in wholemeal baps or pitta bread with crisp lettuce leaves for a tasty lunch-time filler.

As you can see from the above selection tempeh, with a little imagination, can be used in most of your favourite recipes either with meat or instead of it. Try adding sautéed tempeh to a leek and potato pie or to risotto and you will find that your experiment will be well worth the effort for the taste, not to mention the nutritional bonus.

CHAPTER II
Gluten
❧ *(Wheat Protein)* ❧

Wheat gluten is a rich protein food which is mainly used in Japan and China. You can buy it canned in this country disguised with fish and meat-type flavours, but I think this nutritious protein deserves to be recognised as a food in its own right and not as a substitute for other protein foods. It has a meat-like chewiness and its porous texture absorbs flavours from stock, juice, vegetables, herbs and spices. For best results use a strong wholemeal flour. Strong flour comes from hard wheat which contains more protein than soft wheat. You can make gluten from white flour, but using 100 per cent wholemeal means that you not only get a rich protein food but one high in fibre and wheat germ. It makes sense to use wholemeal flour for a more balanced yield.

Gluten has a stretchy, rubbery texture and in bread making it forms pockets in the dough which are then filled with carbon dioxide by the developing yeast. The higher the gluten content of the flour, the lighter the loaf. To release the gluten the dough has to be kneaded. For bread making, 7 to 10 minutes is usually enough, but to extract gluten a longer period of kneading is necessary – approximately 15 to 20 minutes.

Gluten is a high protein food, but not a complete protein (see notes on complete protein, page 6), but as you are unlikely to eat it on its own it is easy to complement it with other protein-rich foods which will balance its amino acid content. Combined with legumes (dried peas, beans and lentils) nuts and seeds or cheese it will achieve the correct balance. When extracted from flour, gluten, which feels sponge-like and should stretch like bubble-gum, is usually precooked before using in a dish. This can be done by either frying, baking, boiling in a savoury stock or steaming. I prefer to fry or bake it as this gives a crispy coating and a firmer texture. It is important to break the gluten rather than cut it before you precook, or the texture will become bread-like rather than chewy. Whatever precooked gluten you do not require will freeze well in polythene bags, so make plenty: then your kneading will be worth the effort and provide several meals. To defrost, simply drop into hot savoury stock and cook for 4 to 5 minutes. After precooking the gluten is ready to either mince, slice or cut into bite-sized pieces to use in a variety of interesting and well-flavoured dishes.

Raw gluten can be moulded with sautéed onion, herbs and spices, formed into thin strips and baked until crisp and brown. These 'ribs' are delicious served with a piquant sauce (see pages 82–3 for Gluten Ribs with Barbecue Sauce). In fact, its uses are extremely variable and I hope my recipes will inspire you to experiment for yourself with this very cheap and nutritious protein.

How to Make Raw Gluten

This quantity will make enough gluten for four meals for four people. I use approximately eight precooked balls for four servings.

900 g/2 lbs strong wholemeal   570 ml/1 pint water
*   flour, plain*

1. Put flour in a large mixing bowl, make a well in the centre and slowly pour water in, mixing as you do so to form a medium-firm unsticky dough.
2. Knead for about 12 to 15 minutes (the longer the better).

Place in a clean bowl, cover and let stand for 45 minutes. Knead dough for a further 15 minutes.

3. Put back into the clean bowl and gently pour cold water over the dough to cover it completely. Let stand for about 4 to 6 hours (you can leave overnight).

4. Now begin to knead and squeeze it under the water as if it were a sponge, being careful to hold the gluten together as you extract the starch. Keep changing the water as it becomes milky from the starch. When the water is almost clear you will have a soft rubbery, pliable ball of raw gluten. Let this drain for 10 minutes.

To Make Fried Gluten Balls
Makes approximately 30

These balls are cooked for only 5 minutes after which they are ready to mince or cut, depending on which recipe you choose.

You will need enough oil, either soya or sunflower, for deep frying.

1. Pour oil in a wok or frying pan and heat on a low temperature or flame.
2. Do not cut the dough but break off pieces to mould into 2.5 cm/1 in balls, making them as round and smooth as possible. When the oil is hot fry only 4 or 5 balls at a time allowing space for them to expand. Baste the balls continuously. They must cook for 5 minutes without browning too much. If cooked too quickly they will not expand, so keep heat at a fairly low temperature.

Country Casserole with Gluten
Serves 4

This is a very simple dish, a good one to start with if you have not used gluten before.

10 fried gluten balls
1 large onion, chopped
1 clove garlic
2 medium to large carrots
3 sticks celery, chopped (using green leaves)
1 good sized green pepper
115 g/4 oz button mushrooms (optional)
1 bay leaf
2 tablespoons fresh parsley,
chopped
1 teaspoon sweet mixed herbs
1 tablespoon wholemeal flour
1 tablespoon tomato purée
610 ml/1¼ pints hot stock or hot water with 1¼ vegetable or beef stock cubes added
170 g/6 oz broad beans (frozen peas will do)
shoyu (naturally fermented soya sauce)

1. Chop the gluten balls into bite-sized pieces.
2. In a medium sized saucepan sauté onion, garlic and carrots for 6 minutes.
3. Add the gluten pieces and fry for 2 minutes.
4. Add celery and green pepper and continue to sauté for 4 more minutes.

5. Stir in mushrooms if using, bay leaf, parsley and herbs and cook for just 1 minute.
6. Add the flour and stirring constantly let cook for 1 minute.
7. Mix tomato purée with stock water and gradually add this to the vegetables and gluten stirring constantly as you do so.
8. Now add the broad beans or peas. Bring to boil then transfer to a casserole dish, cover and bake in the oven, 190°C/375°F/ Gas 5 for 30 to 40 minutes.
9. Finally, stir in the shoyu, but taste before you do so as you might find the flavour delicious without it.

Moussaka with Minced Gluten
Serves 4

This is not an authentic moussaka ('moussaka' means aubergine casserole), but it follows the traditional method with a variation in the ingredients. Instead of minced lamb or beef I have used minced gluten balls. I have also used less aubergines and added courgettes. It still turns out delicious and is quite simple to prepare. Most recipes, including mine until recently, advocated salting the aubergines to get rid of bitter juices, but I have experimented without salt. I simply put sliced aubergines in a colander, place a plate and a weight on top, leave them for 30 minutes, then rinse and pat dry. It seems to work.

10 fried gluten balls
1 large aubergine (about
   225 g/8 oz in weight)
3 large courgettes (about
   450 g/1 lb in weight)
2 medium sized onions (about
   285 g/10 oz in weight)
1 large clove garlic

1 level teaspoon dried marjoram or
   1 tablespoon fresh marjoram,
   chopped
6 medium sized tomatoes, skinned
1 generous tablespoon tomato purée
140 ml/¼ pint stock or hot water
   plus ½ vegetable stock cube
freshly ground black pepper

1. Mince the gluten balls on a coarse cutter.
2. Slice the aubergine thinly, place in a colander, lay a plate with a weight on top and let stand for 30 minutes to get rid of bitter juices.
3. Heat 2 tablespoons of the oil in a pan and sauté onion and garlic for 7 minutes until soft.
4. Stir in the minced gluten and marjoram and sauté for 2 minutes.
5. Blend skinned tomatoes, tomato purée and stock until smooth and pour this over the onions and gluten. Season with a little black pepper. Cover and simmer on low heat for 7 minutes more.
6. Rinse pressed aubergines and pat dry.
7. Heat the remaining oil in another pan and sauté the aubergines and courgettes until golden.
8. Oil a large ovenproof dish. Arrange a layer of aubergines and courgettes in the bottom. Spoon a layer of the tomato mixture over these, then another layer of aubergines and courgettes, and so on, finishing with aubergines and courgettes on top.

For the Topping

2 tablespoons gram flour (chick pea flour)

2 eggs

270 ml/½ pint natural yoghurt

1 tablespoon fresh parsley, chopped

sea salt

freshly ground black pepper to taste

1. Beat the eggs lightly, add the yoghurt and beat together again lightly.
2. Gradually mix in the flour, sea salt and black pepper and very finely chopped parsley. If you have a liquidiser or food processor just blend the lot until smooth.
3. Pour over the moussaka and bake in a preheated oven, 180°C/350°F/Gas 4 for 35 to 40 minutes or until golden brown.

Chilli Beans with Minced Gluten
Serves 4

170 g/6 oz dry weight Red
 Kidney Beans
sea salt
8 fried gluten balls (see
 pages 75–6)
2 tablespoons sunflower oil
2 medium onions, chopped
2 cloves garlic, crushed
1 medium to large sized green

pepper, deseeded and chopped
1 rounded teaspoon cayenne or
 chilli powder
1 rounded teaspoon paprika
396 g/14 oz can tomatoes, well
 chopped
2 tablespoons tomato purée
Surinam brown rice, to serve
fresh green salad, to serve

1. Soak beans overnight, changing the water three times. Rinse and boil vigorously in fresh water for 10 minutes. Turn down to simmer, cover and cook for 40 to 50 minutes more. Do not overcook. Add a little sea salt 10 minutes before the end of cooking time. Drain.
2. Mince the gluten balls.
3. Heat oil in a large heavy-based saucepan. Sauté onion and garlic for 7 minutes. Stir in the minced gluten and continue to fry for 2 minutes.
4. Add green pepper and sauté for 3 more minutes.
5. Stir in the spices and fry for 1 minute.
6. Lastly, add the tomatoes, purée, drained beans and a little sea salt. Stir well and cook for 20 minutes with lid on.

Serve with Surinam brown rice (a thin rice which cooks in 25 minutes) and a fresh green salad.

Simple Gluten Curry
Serves 4

This very simple curry sauce also goes well with fish, but here I
have used thinly sliced gluten balls which absorb the flavours of
the spices and taste quite delicious. If you cannot obtain
coconut milk, use half and half goat's or cow's milk and water
plus 1 teaspoon honey.

10 fried gluten balls	½ teaspoon black mustard seeds, ground
1 large onion, chopped	½ cinnamon stick
2 large cloves garlic, crushed	1 rounded teaspoon rice or
3 tablespoons sunflower oil	wholemeal flour
1 finely chopped fresh chilli or ½ teaspoon chilli powder	285 ml/½ pint canned coconut milk
1 level teaspoon ground coriander	1 tablespoon lemon juice
½ teaspoon turmeric	sea salt to taste
½ teaspoon ground cumin	

1. Slice the gluten balls in thin strips. Sauté onion and garlic in
   the oil for 10 minutes.
2. Add chilli and spices and fry on low heat for 2 minutes.
3. Stir in the gluten strips and sauté for 2 minutes more on low
   heat.
4. Mix flour, coconut milk and lemon juice together and pour
   over the curry mixture.
5. Season with a little sea salt to your own taste.
6. Simmer on low heat with lid on for 20 minutes.

Serve with rice or wholemeal chapatis and a chunky vegetable
salad to which you could add 2 tablespoons of chutney. My
chunky salad consists of steamed and cubed potatoes, chopped
carrots, lightly cooked French beans, peas or sweetcorn, diced
cucumber, a little chopped red pepper and onion, and chutney.
Plain yoghurt is also a refreshing accompaniment with any
curry dish.

Moh-Moh Dumplings with Minced Gluten
Makes 10 – serves 3 to 4

This recipe is adapted from a traditional Tibetan delicacy which I first found in the *Odiyan Country Cook Book* by Bill Farthing. Usually the dumplings are stuffed with meat and served in meat-based soup, but I have experimented with various fillings such as minced steamed tempeh, soya mince, beans and vegetables, and, for a sweet delight, apple, raisin and cinnamon. All have been greatly enjoyed.

To make the dumplings is a knack well worth practising. If using gluten filling as in this recipe it is best to use frozen gluten balls which are easily defrosted by simmering in a good savoury stock for a few minutes. This cuts down the preparation time for this dish enormously.

10 fried gluten balls
2 tablespoons sunflower oil
2 cloves garlic
½ teaspoon fresh grated ginger (optional)
1 heaped teaspoon tomato purée
1 tablespoon fresh chopped parsley or coriander leaves

55 g/2 oz each of minced onion, celery, mushrooms and red pepper
1 tablespoon shoyu (naturally fermented soya sauce)
few drops Tabasco sauce, to your own taste
55 g/2 oz roughly ground almonds

For the Moh-Moh Dough
285 g/10 oz 81 per cent wheatmeal flour, plain
½ teaspoon sea salt
about 250 ml/9 fl oz water

1. Mince the gluten balls coarsely.
2. Heat oil in a pan and over low heat sauté the minced gluten with the garlic for just 1 minute. Stir in the ginger, tomato purée, parsley or coriander and minced vegetables. Cook for 2 minutes only.
3. Add the shoyu, Tabasco and almonds and mix well in. Cool the mixture by placing a piece of muslin in a colander and

spooning the mixture into this. You will get a little juice dripping. Save this for your stock pot.

To Make the Dough

1. Put flour and salt in a mixing bowl and stir in the water.
2. Form into a dough and knead in the bowl for 1 minute.
3. Knead the dough for 2 minutes more with lightly floured hands.
4. Roll the dough with your hands into a sausage shape and cut into 10 equal portions. Place these in a polythene bag so that the dough does not dry out as you roll each piece out.
5. Roll each piece into a ball with your hands and flatten the ball on your working surface. Roll into a small circle approximately 6 cm/2½ in in diameter. Flatten the edges so that the centre is thicker to hold the filling. Hold the circle of dough cupped in one hand and fill the centre with about 1 tablespoon of the cold mixture.
6. Pinch the edges of the dough into thin pleats and stretch pleated edges up over the filling, twisting them knoblike together at the top. Flatten the knob which will then look like a little flattened doughnut.
7. Grease a steamer and place the stuffed dumplings into this and steam for 20 minutes.

These are delicious served with most sauces and great in soups. I often can't resist eating one all on its own!

Gluten Ribs with Barbecue Sauce
Serves 4

For this recipe, I use raw gluten and mould this with warm oil, seasoning, sautéed onion and sunflower seed spread. The warm oil breaks down the gluten and helps the seasoning to penetrate.

340 g/12 oz raw gluten
2 tablespoons sunflower oil
1 medium onion, chopped
1 clove garlic, crushed
2 tablespoons shoyu (naturally

fermented soya sauce)
4 tablespoons sunflower oil
  (warm)
570 ml/1 pint Barbecue Sauce (see
  pages 69–70)

1. Heat the oil in a pan and sauté the onion and garlic over a low heat until transparent, about 10 minutes.
2. Put gluten in a bowl, add sautéed onion and garlic, and put shoyu and warm oil on top.
3. Mould all together with your hands until well merged.
4. Break (do not cut) off pieces of the mixture and form each piece into strips 2.5 × 7.5 cm/1 × 3 in long and just under 1.25 cm/½ in thick. Use hands to do this, twisting and flattening the gluten as you shape the ribs.
5. Place on a well-oiled baking tray. Spoon a little oil on top of the ribs as you would when roasting potatoes. Bake uncovered at 180°C/350°F/Gas 4 for about 35 to 40 minutes, turning them over when brown on the bottom.

When baked, pour over the Barbecue Sauce and bake for a further 10 minutes.

Note: you could top with a little grated cheese before cooking.

CHAPTER III
Goat's Milk Dairy Produce

In many parts of the world the goat is still the main source of milk, cheese and meat. Throughout history goats have been favoured by nomadic tribes because of their ability to forage and obtain nourishment from almost barren land, whereas cattle would find survival in similar harsh conditions extremely difficult, if not impossible. Therefore the goat has generally been a most valued animal.

In the East a man's wealth was gauged by the size of his herd of goats. And in ancient Greece and Rome the cheese made from goat's milk was a favourite food and an essential part of a soldier's diet. During the Roman occupation of Britain the invaders developed the making of goat's cheese in this country. And of course there is Pan – half man, half goat – the chief rural divinity in Greek mythology.

In this country with the speedy advance of the industrial revolution in the eighteenth century a massive move towards the city factories was made by country dwellers who had previously worked on the land. At the same time there was an enormous increase in the demand for milk, meat and leather goods. It is then that the cow, because of its greater size and higher productivity, became more popular and goat-rearing declined rapidly.

Fortunately in recent years there has been a revival of interest in rearing goats and a growing demand for goat's milk, yoghurt and cheese. Much publicity has been given to the nutritional value and easier digestibility of goat's milk especially for babies, and findings have shown that certain allergy-producing proteins present in cow's milk are non-existent in goat's milk. Many doctors now recommend using goat's milk and its produce as an alternative to dairy produce from the cow for those suffering from eczema, asthma, migraine, stomach ulcers and hay-fever. Research has revealed that in many such cases the symptoms have either been alleviated or the patient has gradually been cured. This does not mean that a cure of these illnesses can be solely attributed to simply cutting out cow's dairy produce and using goat's as an alternative. The whole of one's diet is important to curing any illness. All it means is that goat's milk produce seems to be easier on our digestive systems and is less likely to cause allergic conditions. As already mentioned in the Introduction, I do not feel that we have to cut out any particular food to be healthy unless that food brings adverse effects on the healthy growth of our individual bodies because of the way it is produced, whether it be of vegetable origin or livestock.

Before ever tasting goat's milk I had a preconceived idea that it tasted unpleasantly strong. Five years ago I drank my first glass of fresh, chilled goat's milk brought to our wholefood shop in North Devon by a local producer. I was absolutely amazed at how delicious and delicately sweet it tasted. Leaflets were thrust upon me and samples of natural yoghurt, and the soft and semi-hard goat's cheeses soon became very popular with our customers. What had I been missing all these years! I started to experiment and found that the soft cheese made the most delicious cheesecake and cheese sauces, while slices of semi-hard cheese tasted great in lasagne and in pizza. In fact, it enhanced my cooking tremendously. I can't start the day now without a cup of goat's milk yoghurt.

Since that time there has been a very noticeable growth in the number of suppliers and in a demand for goat's milk and goat's milk products in the surrounding area where we still live.

What is so good about goat's milk? Unlike most cows today, goats are free range, that is they live naturally and feed on wild herbage from beet leaves to nettles and thistles, and produce a milk richer in vitamins and minerals than cows. The milk also has smaller fat globules than cow's, making it more digestible, and it has none of the allergy-producing proteins present in cow's milk. 'Factory' cows are now the main producers of our milk, cheese and meat today. They are not only fed on manufactured foodstuffs but are injected with fattening hormones. The result is that their milk, cheese and meat contain residual antibiotics.

Goats are highly unlikely to catch tuberculosis, brucellosis or meleteuses, whereas cows not only can catch these diseases but can transmit them through their milk to humans. For this reason, cow's milk has to be pasteurised which destroys valuable nutrients and enzymes. Goat's milk can be drunk fresh with all its nourishing properties intact. It is now advocated that goat's milk is preferable to cow's milk for weaning babies. Many babies have been found to become sensitised to cow's milk during this weaning period with resulting allergies. Had they been given goat's milk an immunity would have been set up which would have allowed them to include cow's dairy produce in their diet at a later stage. Goat's milk has better keeping properties than cow's milk and takes longer to 'turn'. Also because of its molecular structure, it freezes well, though it is not advisable to store it frozen longer than three months.

Taking all these factors into consideration, I think the hardy goat deserves to be more widely recognised and bred for its nutritionally valuable produce.

Goat's Cheese-Making

I have been greatly assisted in writing this chapter by local producers, especially Sally Hughes who makes the most delicious goat's milk products and sells her natural yoghurts, soft cheese and the tastiest pressed soft cheese, delicately flavoured with parsley and garlic, to our local shops in North Devon. Sally's recipes for making these delights are all here for you to enjoy, plus a few other simple traditional ones that can be made without specialist equipment except for a dairy thermometer and a small cheese press. The press is not essential because you can improvise very easily as described on pages 93–4. An address for suppliers of the diary thermometer and the cheese press is on page 140.

A 'starter' culture is necessary in most cheese-making except for paneer (lemon cheese) or naturally sour milk-curd cheese. Although heat-treating milk has to be done to eliminate undesirable bacteria, it destroys the cheese-making properties in untreated milk. The 'starter' culture reintroduces these and a healthy ripening of the curd is ensured. The 'starter' is milk which contains a special bacterial culture which produces acid during the process of cheese-making. This bacteria feeds on the milk sugar, lactose, and changes it to lactic acid. You can obtain the starter culture from an agricultural college or by mail order from the address given on page 140.

Most cheeses also require rennet. You can use junket rennet but it is not as efficient as cheese-making rennet which is stronger. Rennet is an enzyme which comes from the stomach lining of a suckling animal and coagulates the milk. The discovery of rennet, it is said, probably dates back from the times when milk was carried in bags made from calves' stomachs where the enzyme was still alive and coagulated the milk as it travelled. You can use vegetable rennet with equal success. For addresses of where to obtain both rennets see page 140.

This first recipe for paneer (lemon cheese) is not strictly a cheese at all, but in making it you will become familiar with what is involved in making other cheeses. As milk and lemons are easily available, I think it is a good recipe to start with. You can use cow's milk if you wish. This 'cheese' is much favoured in India where it originated. It is used with various spices in different parts of the country.

Paneer (Fresh Lemon Cheese)

This recipe makes approximately 280 g/10 oz soft curds and about 225 g/8 oz lightly pressed curds.

Equipment

1 stainless steel, iron or enamel pot	*1 colander*
2/3 layers of muslin (or cheesecloth)	*bowl for fitting colander in*
	string to tie up muslin

Ingredients

1.1 litres/2 pints goat's milk	*45 ml/3 tablespoons lemon juice*

1. Bring the milk to the boil, and as soon as it bubbles around the edge and is just beginning to rise take off heat and quickly stir in the lemon juice.
2. Let stand for 15 minutes. The milk will curdle almost immediately.
3. Drape the 2 layers of muslin over a colander which should just fit snugly onto the rim of your bowl or bucket.
4. After standing, strain the curds and whey through the muslin, then lift up the edges of the muslin, tie them together to form a bundle and hang from a tap spout over the bowl in the sink overnight.
5. When well drained, remove cheese from the muslin. You can use it as it is, with different savoury or sweet flavours such as garlic and herbs, sea salt and freshly ground black pepper or dried soaked or fresh fruit.
6. I like to press this cheese lightly, and for this a 6 lb weight is necessary. Wrap curds loosely in the muslin. Fold another piece of muslin in four. Put this on a board or strong plate

with the wrapped cheese on top. Then place a 6 lb weight on top of this. Leave for five hours. The cheese will now be sliceable and can be cut into small squares, sautéed and added to many dishes such as stir-fried vegetables with sweet and sour sauce or any vegetable and sauce dish. Like tofu it does not have much flavour of its own but is a good protein food and absorbs other flavours easily. You could use pressed lemon cheese instead of tofu in most of the tofu recipes given in the book.

This cheese has a short life and should be stored in the refrigerator and eaten within two days.

Lactic Curd Cheese
Yields 450 g/1 lb

This cheese is easily digestible and a good food for infants and invalids. It does not require rennet but needs a starter to sour the milk. The process in making is very simple, but it takes three days to make the cheese because of the long hanging time.

Equipment

dairy thermometer   large bowl to set milk
stainless steel, iron or enamel   large square of cotton sheeting
  saucepan   large square of muslin

Ingredients

2.2 litres/4 pints goat's milk   sea salt (optional)
1 tablespoon starter culture

1. Heat milk to 71°C/160°F and cool quickly to 32°C/90°F by placing saucepan in a sink of cold water.
2. Stir in the starter, mix well for approximately 1 minute.

3. Cover and leave in the airing cupboard for 24 hours. Heat gently to 38°C/100°F and leave for 30 minutes.
4. Turn this into the cotton sheeting, tie edges and hang to drain for 24 hours.
5. Add a little sea salt to the curds if you wish just before turning them into the muslin cloth. Tie edges and hang for a further 24 hours.

This cheese freezes well, and is good in both savoury and sweet dishes.

Scottish Crowdie
Yields 250 g/9 oz

This is a type of cottage cheese, but does not look like cottage cheese as we buy it. Traditionally cottage cheese is not lumpy but has a soft, smooth texture. It is usually made with skimmed milk, but whole goat's milk is fine to use.

Equipment
dairy thermometer   *muslin*
stainless steel saucepan   *colander*
long-handled knife   *perforated ladle*

Ingredients
1.1 litres/2 pints goat's milk   *with 2 tablespoons cold boiled*
2 tablespoons starter culture   *water*
¼ teaspoon cheese rennet diluted   *sea salt (optional)*

1. Heat milk to 71°C/160°F and cool quickly to 29°C/85°F by placing the saucepan in a sink of cold water.
2. Stir in the starter and the diluted rennet. Mix well, cover and leave in the airing cupboard for about 2 to 2½ hours.
3. When set, cut the curds into small cubes.
4. Heat cut curds to 32°C/90°F, stirring constantly. Let stand for 12 minutes.

5. Drape muslin over the colander and ladle the curds into the muslin. Hang to drain for about 4 hours.
6. Place cheese in a bowl and add a little sea salt at this stage if you wish.

It will last three days maximum in the fridge. It is delicious with chives, red pepper, little chopped gherkins or with chopped pineapple or other soaked, dried or fresh fruit.

Sally Hughes' Soft Cheese
Yields 450 g/1 lb

Absolutely delicious and very simple to make. Sally uses only 1 tablespoon starter, 3 to 4 drops of rennet when making double this quantity, with equal success.

Equipment

dairy thermometer
large stainless steel saucepan
bowl for setting the milk
colander
muslin and string to tie muslin
bowl or small bucket that colander will fit snugly into to catch the whey
perforated ladle

Ingredients

2.2 litres/4 pints goat's milk
1 tablespoon starter culture
3 to 4 drops cheese rennet

1. Heat milk to boiling point (just beginning to rise up the pan).
2. Cool quickly, by placing the saucepan in a sink of cold water, to 32°C/90°F and pour into a scalded bowl.
3. Stir in 1 tablespoon starter and three drops of cheese rennet.
4. Mix well for 1 minute. Cover and place in the airing cupboard for 15 to 18 hours. By then you will have a fairly solid mass.

5. Drape the muslin over a scalded colander. Place this over a deep bowl or small household bucket in which the colander fits snugly.
6. Carefully ladle the curds into the muslin. Gather the edges of the muslin, tie muslin and hang to drip in a fairly cool place for 18 hours.
7. When the cheese has drained enough, remove from the muslin, wrap in cling film and refrigerate until needed.

Sally does not salt the cheese. A good idea from her is to put some of the cheese into individual containers and flavour these little cheeses with either fresh chopped herbs, chives cut small with kitchen scissors, garlic and chopped parsley, nuts and raisins, celery seeds, green and red peppers, fresh chopped pineapple or mandarin oranges.

The cheese will keep for at least 1 week in the refrigerator.

Sally Hughes' Pressed Soft Cheese

Taking Sally's previous recipe for soft cheese, but doubling up on the ingredients (4.41 litres/8 pints milk yields 450 g/1 lb), you can make a firmer cheese, either plain or flavoured, by pressing in a cheese press for about 12 hours. A small cheese press (see diagram) can be obtained by mail order from the address given on page 140.

You can improvise, however. Either use a small 15 cm/6 in cake tin or a large can, such as holds 794 g/1 lb 12 oz tomatoes (cleaned and sterilised) with holes drilled in the sides. You will also need a round, smooth, well-seasoned piece of wood (called a follower) which is just smaller than the tin in diameter and about 3.2 kg/7 lb in weight.

Sally makes a delicious parsley and garlic moulded cheese and adds the finely chopped and minced garlic just before pressing.

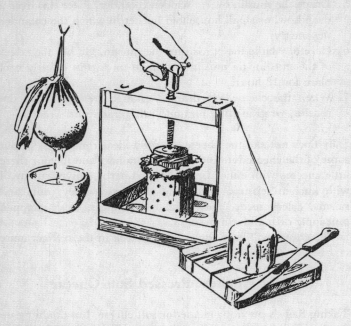

1. Line your scalded tin with a damp piece of butter muslin and pack in the soft cheese.
2. Fold the muslin over the cheese, place the wooden follower on top and then the weight. Let stand for 12 hours. You will only get a little whey so place the tin in a shallow dish while the cheese is firming. When pressed enough, remove the muslin, wrap in cling film and refrigerate. It will keep for 1 week. Try roughly ground black pepper pressed around the edge of this cheese, toasted crushed almonds, or walnut halves, etc. for a change in flavour.

When you have mastered these simple cheeses there is a fund of information to be had from specialist books on the subject. The Goat Society are most helpful if you would like to develop the art of goat's milk cheese-making further; their address is given on page 140.

Goat's Milk Yoghurt and Yoghurt Cheese

About Yoghurt

Many therapeutic benefits have been attributed to yoghurt, but no food is a wonder cure all by itself. A balanced diet which includes a variety of health-giving food as pure and as fresh as possible is more important than latching on to one particular food. Yoghurt does deserve a regular place in our diet. There has been much research into the claimed curative properties of yoghurt. Findings have shown that the bacteria in yoghurt kill harmful bacteria in the large intestine, because they turn milk sugar (lactose) into lactic acid and the harmful bacteria cannot live in lactic acid. The bacteria in yoghurt can also manufacture B vitamins in the intestine. Those who are taking antibiotics, which are known to cause vitamin deficiency, would be well advised to eat yoghurt regularly.

You can make your own yoghurt very simply using either a dried starter culture or a commercial natural yoghurt. Most bought yoghurt contains two varieties of bacteria, Laelobacillus bulgaricus and streptococcus, which complement each other in growing, but read the label carefully. If it has stabilisers in it, then it is not a live food and will not make yoghurt. If you follow these directions carefully you will have perfect yoghurt every time. There are, however, some important points to remember. If the developing yoghurt is exposed to too high a heat it will separate and turn sour and be bitter tasting. If cheesy in taste, then it may have stray bacteria in it so make sure to sterilise all utensils and use a fresh starter when making the next batch. And finally, if the starter culture does not work at all then it could be that the temperature of the milk was wrong when adding the starter. It should be around 43°C/110°F because at 49°C/120°C the bacteria will die and under 35°C/95°F they become inactive. Sally, who makes a superb goat's milk yoghurt, lowers the temperature of the boiled milk to 46°C/115°F, pours it into a jug and then stirs in the yoghurt culture. By the time the milk has been poured into the jug it is probably about 43°C/110°F.

You can buy various yoghurt-making gadgets or use a wide necked vacuum flask which keeps a constant temperature. You can also make very successful yoghurt in a jug or deep bowl as long as you cover it, wrap it in a thick, warm towel and leave it in the airing cupboard. Sally suggests pouring the yoghurt into plastic pots with lids placing these in large plastic boxes surrounded with polystyrene beads, covering and placing in the airing cupboard. Simmering the milk for 20 minutes will give you a thicker yoghurt as it concentrates the milk.

How to Make Goat's Milk Yoghurt

1.1 litres/2 pints goat's milk   *1 tablespoon natural yoghurt*
dried yoghurt culture or

1. Boil the milk until it reaches 88°C/190°F. Maintain the milk at simmering point for 20 minutes on low heat.
2. Now put a lid on the saucepan to stop a hard skin forming and place the saucepan in a sink or large bowl of cold water to cool as quickly as possible to approximately 46°C/115°F.
3. Pour in a large sterilised jug and stir in either the dried culture (follow directions on packet for adding) or the tablespoon of natural yoghurt. Stir well with a plastic spatula or a long plastic spoon.
4. Pour either into thermos flasks, a yoghurt maker, plastic pots surrounded by polystyrene beads as previously suggested, or just leave in the jug, cover, wrap in a warm towel and place in the airing cupboard. Keep the developing yoghurt in as constant a temperature as possible. It will take about 6 hours to set. When set, refrigerate immediately.

How to Make Goat's Milk Yoghurt Cheese

All you need is a piece of muslin and some cord to tie the dripping yoghurt up with. Spread the muslin over a colander, pour the fresh yoghurt into this, twist and tie the edges with the cord. Hang over a pot and let drip for 4 to 8 hours. The longer you let it drip the thicker the cheese will be.

Paneer (Lemon Cheese) with Spiced Mushrooms, Tomato and Green Pea Sauce
Serves 4

For this recipe you can use up some of the whey which adds both nutritional value and flavour to the sauce. You need quite a bit of oil to sauté the paneer as it sticks to the pan easily. A non-stick pan is best to use.

225 g/8 oz paneer (pressed)
5 tablespoons sunflower oil
1 medium sized onion, chopped
1 clove garlic
1 small green pepper, deseeded and
   chopped
1 fresh green chilli, deseeded and
   finely chopped
1 level teaspoon ground coriander
1 level teaspoon ground cumin
½ teaspoon turmeric
¼ teaspoon clove powder

1 level teaspoon methi (fenugreek
   leaf)
1 level teaspoon freshly grated
   ginger root
½ cinnamon stick
6 medium sized ripe tomatoes,
   skinned and chopped
425 ml/¾ pint whey and
   1 teaspoon sea salt
175 g/6 oz small button
   mushrooms
340 g/12 oz frozen peas

1. Cut paneer into 2.5 cm/1 in squares.
2. Heat the oil in the pan over a medium heat. Sauté the paneer until golden brown on both sides. Remove paneer with a fish slice and put aside on a plate.
3. Sauté the onion and garlic in the same oil until soft, about 5 minutes.

4. Add the green pepper and continue to fry for 3 minutes more.
5. Now add all the chilli and spices and fry on a low heat, stirring constantly for 2 minutes.
6. Stir in the tomatoes, whey and sea salt.
7. Cook gently with lid on for 5 minutes. Remove cinnamon stick.
8. Place the sauce in a liquidiser or food processor and blend until smooth.
9. Return sauce to the pan and stir in the mushrooms and defrosted peas.
10. Place the sautéed paneer squares gently in the mixture one by one. Cover pan and cook on gentle heat for 7 minutes only.

This is delicious served with plain brown rice or chapatis.

Another way to serve fried paneer is with Leeks and Mushrooms with Soya Bean Sprouts (see page 132 for recipe). All you do is follow the recipe for the sautéed vegetables and spoon over the sautéed paneer squares. This makes a very tasty lunch or late supper dish accompanied by wholemeal French bread.

Courgette and Mushroom Quiche with Lactic Curd or Sally's Soft Cheese

This will fill a 22.5 cm/9 in flan dish and the variations are endless (see end of recipe).

1 quantity short crust pastry (see page 35)
3 tablespoons sunflower oil
225 g/8 oz courgettes, thinly sliced into rings
1 small onion, cut into thin rings
55 g/2 oz small button mushrooms, thinly sliced
175 ml/6 fl oz goat's, cow's or soya milk

30 ml/2 tablespoons natural yoghurt
115 g/6 oz Lactic Curd or Soft Cheese
3 large eggs or 4 medium eggs
¼ teaspoon ground mace
¼ teaspoon mustard powder

¼ teaspoon freshly ground black pepper
sea salt to taste
a little oregano, and a sprinkling of dried tarragon or any herbs you like to top the filling

1. Line the oiled flan dish with the pastry and bake blind in a preheated oven for 10 minutes at 190°C/375°F/Gas 5. Let cool.
2. Heat oil in a pan and sauté the courgettes and onion for 4 minutes only.
3. Add the mushrooms and sauté for 2 minutes more. Let cool.
4. Whisk milk, yoghurt and cheese together until well blended.
5. Whisk eggs with mace, mustard, black pepper and sea salt.
6. Whisk milk and egg mixtures together.
7. Spoon courgette mixture into the cooled flan case, pour over the egg mixture and sprinkle the herbs on top. Bake at 190°C/375°F/Gas 5 on middle shelf of the oven for 40 minutes or until slightly risen and golden brown on top. Pierce centre with a fork and let stand for 7 minutes before cutting.

Leek and Lactic Curd or Soft Cheese Quiche

Simply substitute 285 g/10 oz of leeks for the courgettes, mushrooms and onion in the previous recipe. Cut the leeks after trimming into 6 cm/¼ in thin rings (use as much of the soft green part as possible), sauté these in a little olive oil or sunflower oil for 10 minutes with the lid on the pan. Cool and proceed as for Courgette and Mushroom Quiche.

Spring Onion Quiche with Lactic Curd or Soft Cheese

Substitute 1 large bunch of spring onions for the vegetables used in the previous quiches. Chop and sauté these in either olive oil or sunflower oil, for just one minute. Leave out the herbs and mace and sprinkle a little freshly ground nutmeg on top.

Greek Spiced Onion Quiche

1 quantity short crust pastry, see page 35

For the Filling

2 medium sized bunches of large spring onions
2 tablespoons olive or sunflower oil
1 rounded teaspoon caraway seeds
few drops Tabasco sauce
little sea salt and freshly ground

black pepper
200 ml/8 fl oz natural yoghurt or milk
170 g/6 oz Lactic Curd or Sally's soft cheese
3 small eggs

1. Line an oiled 22.5 cm/9 in flan dish with the pastry. Prick the base and bake blind for 10 minutes. Cool.
2. Roughly chop the spring onions using the green ends. Sauté in the oil for 1 minute with the caraway seeds, Tabasco, sea salt and black pepper. Cool.
3. Whisk the yoghurt, cheese and eggs together.
4. Stir the cooled onion mixture into this and then pour into the baked, cooled flan case. Bake at 200°C/400°F/Gas 6 for 10 minutes then turn down the heat to 180°C/350°F/Gas 4 for a further 20 minutes.

Delicious hot or cold.

Pierogi

These miniature pasties originated from Poland and are made from a rich cheese pastry and filled with mushrooms. They make a lovely party dish and are delicious eaten hot or cold.

225 g/8 oz polyunsaturated margarine
115 g/4 oz Sally's Soft Cheese
1 egg, beaten
450 g/1 lb 81 per cent wheatmeal

flour
1 level teaspoon sea salt
egg for glazing and sealing edges of pasties

For the Filling

1 large onion (about 225 g/8 oz), very finely chopped
3 tablespoons olive oil
1 teaspoon marjoram
3 slices wholemeal bread soaked in a little white wine
450 g/1 lb small button

mushrooms, washed, well dried and finely chopped
2 eggs, hard-boiled
4 tablespoons natural yoghurt
sea salt and plenty of freshly ground black pepper to taste

1. First make the pastry. Cream the margarine and cheese together, add the beaten egg with 1 tablespoon of the flour and cream it in.
2. Sieve the remaining flour with the salt and gradually add to the creamed mixture. Form into a soft dough, place in a plastic bag and refrigerate overnight, or for 1 hour.
3. To make the filling, sauté the onion in olive oil with the lid on until soft.
4. Add the marjoram and sauté for another 2 minutes. Remove from the heat.
5. Mash the soaked bread and stir into the mushrooms.
6. Sieve the hard-boiled eggs and add the yoghurt, sea salt and black pepper. Allow to cool before filling the pasties.
7. Roll out the dough on a well-floured surface. (Place a plastic sheet over the dough as you roll. This helps to stop it sticking

and prevents the addition of too much flour which will dry out this delicious pastry.) Roll out to .3 cm/⅛ in thick. Using a plain-edged pastry cutter, 8 cm/3 in in diameter, cut out 30 circles. Place a heaped teaspoon of the filling in the centre of each circle. Egg brush the edges, fold up to the centre and press gently together. Brush the tops with egg and bake at 190°C/375°F/Gas 5 for 15 minutes until golden brown.

Double Pizza Pie With
Sally's Pressed Soft Cheese
Makes 8 portions

This recipe uses pizza dough on top of the filling as well as the bottom. I use an oval shallow pie dish approximately 32.5 cm/13 in long and 20 cm/8 in wide but you can use any shape as long as the volume is similar. You can vary the vegetables according to what is in season or what you fancy.

1 quantity pizza dough (see page 33)
2 good sized onions, chopped
2 large cloves garlic
3 tablespoons olive oil or sunflower oil
1 large green pepper, chopped
2 medium sized courgettes, sliced
6 medium sized tomatoes, skinned and chopped
2 tablespoons tomato purée
1 teaspoon dried basil
little sea or herb salt and freshly ground black pepper to taste
10 black olives, stoned and halved
340 g/12 oz pressed Soft Cheese
little beaten egg to brush edges and top of dough

1. As the dough rises sauté the onion and garlic in the oil in a pan for 7 minutes.
2. Add the green pepper and courgettes and continue to fry for 5 minutes more.
3. Stir in the chopped tomatoes, tomato purée, basil, sea or herb salt and black pepper. Let cook gently with the lid

slightly off for 5 minutes to evaporate some of the liquid. Then stir in the olives.

4. Knead the risen dough for 2 minutes. Break in half and roll out each half to fit the size of your tin. (The dough must not be too thick.)

5. Place one half onto the well-oiled dish or tin. Crumble on half the cheese leaving 2.5 cm/1 in from the edge. Spoon on the vegetable mixture and another layer of crumbled cheese. Brush egg on the edge of the pizza dough. Top with the other half of the pizza dough, pressing edges together.

6. Cut 3 × 5cm/2 in slits in the centre of the dough and brush with egg. Bake in preheated oven, 200°C/400°F/Gas 6 for 10 minutes. Turn down heat to 190°C/375°F/Gas 5 and continue to bake for 20 minutes more.

This pie lends itself to many variations. Tofu or tempeh can be used, with less cheese. Chopped spinach or Swiss chard added to the cooked sauce is delicious. Aubergine slices or artichoke hearts sliced add an exotic touch. In fact, try whatever you fancy.

Parsley Pancakes with Soft Cheese and Rich Italian Sauce
Serves 5

sea salt and freshly ground black pepper
285 g/10 oz Sally's Soft Cheese
1 quantity Parsley Pancakes (see pages 65–6)
1 quantity Rich Italian Sauce (see pages 25–6)
55 g/2 oz pumpkin seeds for topping

1. Mix a little sea salt and freshly ground black pepper into the cheese.

2. Divide the cheese into 10 equal portions and fill the pancakes with them.

3. Roll up pancakes and place in a well-oiled large ovenproof dish.
4. Heat sauce. Liquidise if you like and pour over the pancakes.
5. Sprinkle on the pumpkin seeds and bake at 200°C/400°F/ Gas 6 for 15 minutes.

A variation of this recipe is to fill the pancakes with the Rich Italian Sauce to which you add 115 g/4 oz roughly ground hazelnuts or almonds and make a soft or curd cheese white sauce using 115 g/4 oz cheese, 650 ml/1 ¼ pints milk to 30 g/1 oz unbleached white flour. Pour this over the stuffed pancakes, top with a little grated Parmesan cheese and a sprinkling of oregano. Bake at 190°C/375°F/Gas 5 for 25 minutes, or until cheese has browned on top.

Courgettes Stuffed with Cheese and Mushrooms
Serves 4

You can use either Scottish Crowdie, Sally's Soft Cheese or Lactic Curd.

6 medium sized courgettes, approximately 18 cm/7 in long
3 tablespoons sunflower oil
1 medium onion, very finely chopped (almost minced)
1 small red pepper, very finely chopped (almost minced)
1 clove garlic, crushed
115 g/4 oz button mushrooms, thinly sliced
½ level teaspoon freshly ground coriander seeds
225 g/8 oz either Crowdie,

Sally's Soft Cheese, or Lactic Curd cheese
¼ level teaspoon cayenne pepper or chilli powder
sea salt to taste
1 tablespoon very finely chopped parsley
2 large egg yolks
230 ml/8 fl oz natural yoghurt
1 level tablespoon gram flour (chick pea flour)
55 g/2 oz ground sesame seeds

1. Steam the whole courgettes until slightly tender only. Let cool.
2. Slice in half lengthwise and spoon out the seedy pulp leaving enough flesh on the skins to keep courgette boats firm enough to stuff.
3. Chop the pulp very finely and leave to one side in a bowl.
4. Heat oil in a pan and sauté the onion, red pepper and garlic for 3 minutes only. Take out with a perforated spoon and add to courgette pulp.
5. Cook the mushrooms with the ground coriander in the oil and juices from the sautéed vegetables for 2 minutes. Add to courgette pulp and onion mixture. Cool.
6. Stir the cheese into the cooked vegetables and add the cayenne pepper or chilli powder and sea salt to your taste. (You can use freshly ground black pepper if you do not wish to use cayenne or chilli powder.)
7. Stir in the parsley and spoon this mixture into the courgette boats. Place stuffed courgettes in a lightly oiled ovenproof dish.
8. Whisk egg yolks and then whisk into the natural yoghurt with the gram flour. Season this lightly with a little sea salt.
9. Pour over each stuffed courgette. Sprinkle on the ground sesame seeds. Bake in a preheated oven, 180°C/350°F/Gas 4 for about 20 minutes.

Stuffed Courgettes with Lentil and Cheese Filling
Serves 4

Use 6 medium courgettes steamed, cut and with their pulp removed as in the previous recipe. Reserve the pulp.

170 g/6 oz red split lentils (dry weight)
sea salt
375 ml/⅔ pint water
1 medium onion, finely chopped
1 large clove garlic
2 tablespoons sunflower oil
1 teaspoon crushed fennel seeds
115 g/4 oz button mushrooms
2 tablespoons lemon juice

1 tablespoon very finely chopped parsley
1 egg
115 g/4 oz Sally's Soft, Lactic Curd or Crowdie cheese
freshly ground black pepper
3 tablespoons fine, wholemeal breadcrumbs
2 tablespoons grated Cheddar cheese

1. Wash lentils and cook gently in the water and a little sea salt until soft and all water is absorbed.
2. Sauté onion and garlic in the oil until soft, about 7 minutes.
3. Add the crushed fennel seeds and the mushrooms and sauté for 3 minutes more.
4. Chop the courgette pulp very finely and add to the onion. Stir in the lemon juice and parsley.
5. When the lentils are cooked you should have a fairly firm consistency like mashed potatoes. Stir in the sautéed vegetables and let the mixture cool.
6. Whisk the egg and stir into the cooled lentil mixture. Blend in the cheese and season with sea salt and freshly ground black pepper.
7. Spoon this mixture into the courgette boats.
8. Combine breadcrumbs with the grated cheese and sprinkle over the top of the stuffed courgettes.
9. Place filled courgettes in an oiled baking dish and bake in a preheated oven, 180°C/350°F/Gas 4, for 20 minutes.

Hot Yoghurt Soup

Serves 6 as a starter, 4 as a main meal

In India and the Middle Eastern countries yoghurt is often an ingredient in soups and sauces.

Indian Karhis are lightly spiced soup-like dishes which are thickened with gram flour (chick pea flour). There are many variations of this and they are sometimes eaten plain with boiled rice or have added vegetables. Mixing flour with yoghurt before adding to a soup, stew or sauce will prevent the yoghurt from curdling while cooking. Here I give you my version which includes vegetables, and parsley and cheese dumplings.

My method of cooking this dish is different from the traditional Indian method but it is much appreciated whenever I serve it.

2 tablespoons sunflower oil
1 large onion
2 cloves garlic
1 teaspoon cumin seed
½ teaspoon turmeric
¼ teaspoon clove powder
1 level teaspoon freshly ground
  coriander seeds
1 very level teaspoon freshly grated
  root ginger
1 cinnamon stick
1 fresh chilli, finely chopped

1 rounded teaspoon methi
  (fenugreek leaves)
225 g/8 oz French beans or okra
  (ladies fingers) cut into
  1.25 cm/½ in pieces
6 medium tomatoes, skinned and
  puréed in a blender
850 ml/1½ pints water
1 vegetable stock cube or a little
  sea salt to your taste
2 tablespoons gram flour
340 ml/12 fl oz natural yoghurt

1. Heat the oil in a heavy-based frying pan and sauté the onion and garlic for 10 minutes with lid on.
2. Add all the spices including fresh chilli and methi herb and sauté for 2 minutes more on a low heat, stirring constantly. Take off heat.
3. Stir in beans and tomatoes.

4. In a cup mix gram flour with a little water to make a smooth, runny batter consistency.
5. Whisk yoghurt with a balloon whisk and slowly add 285 ml/ ½ pint of the water until well blended together.
6. Pour the gram flour mixture into this, whisking as you do so.
7. Add the rest of the water.
8. Bring this to boil stirring constantly in a large heavy-based saucepan and stir in the sautéed vegetable and spice mixture.

For the Parsley and Cheese Dumplings

55 g/2 oz polyunsaturated margarine
185 g/6 oz Lactic Curd, Crowdie or Sally's Soft Cheese
55 g/2 oz very finely chopped
parsley
1 egg, beaten
½ teaspoon sea salt
225 g/8 oz 81 per cent wheatmeal flour

1. Put margarine and cheese into a mixing bowl and cream together.
2. Add the parsley and blend in.
3. Add the beaten egg and salt with 2 tablespoons of the flour and cream it in.
4. Gradually add the rest of the flour and form into a soft dough.
5. Place in a plastic bag and refrigerate for 1 hour. When chilled form into small 2.5 cm/1 in balls with floured hands. Add to the soup and simmer on a low heat for 15 minutes.

Pecan Nut Cheese Balls
Serves 4

These are absolutely delicious served with an onion sauce using 850 ml/1½ pints milk, and lightly steamed broccoli, spinach or Swiss chard. You could also try them with recipes using meat balls. I sometimes add them to an Italian Sauce and serve with noodles or spaghetti. You can use walnuts instead of pecans.

170 g/6 oz medium to fine ground pecans
85 g/3 oz wholemeal breadcrumbs
1 small onion, very finely chopped
2 rounded tablespoons finely chopped parsley

1 tablespoon shoyu (naturally fermented soya sauce)
115 g/4 oz Lactic Curd or Sally's Soft Cheese
1 large egg and 2 tablespoons water to bind

1. Mix all ingredients together in a bowl and form into golf ball size pieces.
2. Place in a well-oiled ovenproof dish and cover with the onion sauce and bake for 30 minutes at 190°C/375°F/Gas 5. If adding the balls to an Italian Sauce make them smaller and cook them in the sauce for 20 minutes.

Chilled Mango Cheese Pie

This pie takes 24 hours to set so prepare it the day before it is needed. The ingredients will fill a 23 cm/9 in pie dish.

170 g/6 oz wholewheat digestive biscuits
55 g/2 oz sesame seeds

½ teaspoon ground cinnamon
85 g/3 oz polyunsaturated margarine

For the Filling

340 g/12 oz Sally's Soft Cheese
225 g/9 oz natural yoghurt
4 level tablespoons clear honey

4 drops vanilla essence
finely grated rind of 1 lemon
1 good sized mango
30 g/1 oz flaked toasted almonds

1. Finely crumb the biscuits and mix with seeds and cinnamon.
2. Melt the margarine and stir into the biscuit crumbs.
3. Oil the pie dish and press the biscuit mixture into this.

4. Bake in a preheated oven, 150°C/300°F/Gas 2, for 5 minutes only. Leave to get cold.

To Make the Filling

1. Cream the cheese with the yoghurt and honey until quite smooth.
2. Stir in the vanilla and lemon rind.
3. Peel and chop the mango into small pieces. Stir this into the cheese mixture.
4. Pour this into the prepared biscuit base. Chill for 24 hours. Just before serving, toast the almonds under a low grill until golden and sprinkle them on.

You can use fresh chopped peaches or ripe fresh chopped apricots instead of the mango and substitute toasted chopped hazelnuts or pumpkin seeds for the almonds.

Swiss-Style Baked Yoghurt Cheesecake

This delightful cheesecake which I have only very slightly altered was first served to me 20 years ago in Switzerland. Fruit sugar looks like caster sugar.

1 quantity biscuit base, cold (see page 109)

For the Filling

225 g/8 oz Sally's Soft Cheese or
 Scottish Crowdie
225 g/8 oz yoghurt cheese
85 g/3 oz fruit sugar
4 eggs, separated
juice of ½ lemon
rind of 1 lemon, very finely grated
4 drops vanilla essence

1 tablespoon yoghurt cheese
 to spread on top
fresh strawberries, raspberries or
 sliced fresh ripe apricots to
 decorate. (Soak the apricots for
 1 hour in a little water and
 apple juice concentrate and
 drain before decorating.)

1. Cream the soft cheese, yoghurt cheese and sugar together until smooth, about 3 minutes.
2. Whisk the egg yolks and gradually add the cheese mixture.
3. Stir in the lemon juice, rind and vanilla.
4. Whisk egg whites into stiff peaks.
5. *Fold* them into the cheese mixture.
6. Pour into the prepared biscuit base and bake in a preheated oven, 170°C/325°F/Gas 3 for 1 hour. If it gets too brown on top then cover with a piece of baking foil or greaseproof paper.
7. When quite cold spread on the tablespoon of yoghurt cheese and decorate with the fruit of your choice.

Nut and Yoghurt Ice Crunch
Serves 6

You can use hazelnuts, almonds, walnuts or a mixture of all three for this recipe.

115 g/4 oz nuts
85 g/3 oz Force wholewheat flakes, crushed (these are like cornflakes but more nutritious)
3 egg whites

85 g/3 oz either fruit sugar or soft dark brown
2 tablespoons skimmed milk powder
250 ml/½ pint natural yoghurt

1. Grind the nuts to breadcrumb consistency and toast under the grill on low heat until lightly browned. Let cool in a bowl.
2. Stir in the crushed wholewheat flakes.
3. Whisk egg whites into stiff peaks, then whisk in the sugar.
4. Blend milk powder with the yoghurt until smooth and stir this into the nut mixture.
5. Now fold the nuts and yoghurt mixture into the egg whites and sugar.
6. Put the mixture into a plastic container with a tight lid and

freeze until quite firm. Take out 25 minutes before serving to soften.

Children love this served with fresh fruit salad.

Rich Yoghurt and Fruit Ice Cream
Serves 6

Strictly for special occasions. Puréed raspberries, strawberries, fresh apricots, peaches or nectarines are all equally good in this recipe. If using raspberries then put through a sieve after they have been puréed to remove the seeds. To skin apricots, peaches or nectarines, just blanch in boiling water and peel.

The recipe requires making a rich custard sauce with yoghurt, cream and eggs. This has to be cooked slowly in a double boiler or pan over hot but not boiling water to prevent the yoghurt from curdling.

570 ml/1 pint natural yoghurt
140 ml/¼ pint double cream
3 tablespoons clear honey
2 eggs and 2 egg yolks

few drops of vanilla essence
340 g/12 oz fruit purée of your
choice

1. Blend yoghurt with the cream and honey.
2. Whisk in the eggs and yolks and beat for 1 minute. When well blended, put into a double boiler or saucepan over a pan of hot, but not boiling, water. Stir until the mixture thickens and coats the back of the spoon. Leave to cool.
3. Stir the fruit and vanilla essence into the cooled custard.

Freeze in a plastic container, covered. Let soften in the fridge approximately 30 minutes before serving.

You could try stirring a little Kirsch or other liqueur into the fruit before adding to the custard for that extra special dinner party touch.

CHAPTER IV
❦ *Sprouting Beans, Grains and Seeds* ❧

A nutritious high-protein food either fresh in salads or lightly cooked and available all year round. That is what sprouted seeds can be for us – a marvellous convenience food packed with vitamins and minerals.

As you will have noticed throughout the book, the home-made proteins, except for cheese-making using a starter culture and rennet, have been a main ingredient in Middle Eastern and Far Eastern cuisine for centuries. Bean sprouts have also been an important part of the diet in the East for around 5000 years. In the West we seem to have virtually ignored this valuable food except for the odd spurts of interest in history when for instance a Dr David MacBride in the eighteenth century experimented with sprouted barley seeds, made a wort from these and found it to be a cure for scurvy, a disease which sometimes killed half the crew on long voyages. Captain Cook served this wort to his crew on board the *Endeavour* with the result that not one sailor died from scurvy on its three voyages from 1768 to 1771. Unfortunately, this effective cure was soon ignored when it was found that lemons could also prevent and cure this disease.

Much later, during the Second World War, there was revived interest in sprouting seeds as citrus fruit was not easily available. British and American Governments advised the use of sprouted seeds because of their high protein content. In particular in America in the early 40s when a protein shortage was imminent the Government mounted a nationwide campaign to educate people, not only about sprouting seeds but also to extol the virtues of the soya bean. When the expected shortage did not occur, interest in sprouting seeds and the soya bean sadly dwindled.

Up until the last few years the majority of us in the West had probably only eaten bean sprouts in Chinese restaurants, cooked and doused in soya sauce and monosodium glutamate. But there is at present a growing interest in sprouting seeds. Fortunately one can buy fresh sprouts in most supermarkets and greengrocer shops at an amazingly cheap price. Commercially sold bean sprouts are usually sprouted from the mung bean, but there is a huge variety of beans, grains and seeds which can be easily sprouted at home. Each has its own particular flavour and texture and will not only enhance your cooking but enrich the body with nature's fresh goodness. As they are eaten while still growing there is no nutritional loss; all the minerals and vitamins are still intact in the growing seeds. When vegetables such as spring greens or lettuce are picked they lose approximately 25 per cent of their vitamin C within half an hour. During storage, vegetables gradually lose their nutritional value, so freshness is of prime importance. You can't eat any vegetables fresher than bean sprouts.

Children love to sprout seeds and in doing so they can learn to appreciate all growing plants. I will never forget the first time my daughter sprouted her own seeds: she got so attached to them that she found that batch impossible to eat. Her excitement was tremendous when she saw that when exposed to sunlight the tiny leaves become tinged with green.

Sprouted seeds are more readily digestible and are higher in food value than the dormant seed or plant because of the complex changes which occur in the seed on germination. The proteins, carbohydrates and oils are broken down into more digestible amino acids, natural sugars and fatty acids and there is a huge increase in the quantity of vitamins and amino acids already present in the seed.

Some seeds contain more vitamin C while others contain more of the B-complex vitamins. Vitamin C can be increased by as much as five times more than the amount present in the dry seeds. Significant increases in the B vitamins and the development of B12 occurs in various stages throughout the growth period. In some seeds the vitamin A content can increase by three times more than is present before germination.

Another important change takes place in the sprouting seed which is useful for slimmers: the calorific content is drastically reduced. Fattening starches are changed into less fattening substances. Soya beans which have the highest protein content of all sprouting beans contain 115 calories per 25 g/1 oz before sprouting and only about 12 calories when sprouted.

In their raw state, peas and beans contain substances such as glycosides, saponins, and alkaloids which are harmful to the digestion. When fresh, 5 minutes' cooking will render these substances harmless. When using the dried variety however, proper soaking, rinsing and cooking for the right length of time are needed to stop any action of the poisonous substances.

The soya bean, which has a high level of these substances, also contains a trypsin inhibitor which prevents the body assimilating an important amino acid called methionine. For this reason it has in the past been strongly advised to cook sprouted soya beans before eating. But recent research has revealed that the inhibitors present in the raw peas and beans, including the soya bean, are eliminated when germination takes place.

The length of time each seed requires to grow and be eaten at its nutritional best varies from 2 to 7 days. The sprouting chart will give you guidelines, but remember that the temperature in which seeds germinate will affect their growth.

About the Beans and Seeds to Sprout

You can buy seed sprouters which have three tiers and allow you to sprout individual seeds or beans separately and also ensure that your seeds and beans do not sit in stagnant water. You can however successfully sprout using a glass jar, a piece of muslin and an elastic band. I will list just some of the more popular beans and seeds with their nutritional value which can be sprouted but there is a huge variety to choose from once you begin sprouting your own.

You might wonder why, when you start to grow your own sprouts, they are not long and straight like commercially bought ones. Well, roots grow downwards so the jar method of growing sprouts means each time the seeds are rinsed they are disturbed and the roots curl and twist about to find their way down. Commercially grown beansprouts are grown in huge containers and are never disturbed as they are rinsed by having water poured over the top and drained through tiny holes at the bottom of the containers. I will give you two methods of sprouting to enable you to sprout longer, straight sprouts.

You will be amazed at the bulk of fresh produce you end up with after sprouting just a handful of seeds or beans. Just 55 g/2 oz of mung beans for instance will yield 225 g/8 oz fresh bean sprouts, nearly the size of the commercial packs available which hold 280 g/10 oz.

Here is a list of my favourite beans and seeds which are both simple to sprout and delicious in a variety of fresh and cooked dishes.

Sprouting Beans

Aduki Beans
Named 'The King of Beans' by the Japanese. Originating from Japan these little red beans have been widely used there and in China for centuries for culinary and medicinal purposes. The juice from the cooked bean is said to be a cure for kidney complaints. Not only are they tasty when sprouted but they are delicious soaked and cooked in rissole shape with bulgur wheat, or as a protein base for shepherds' pie. The sprouted seeds contain around 25 per cent protein and are rich in vitamin C and the B vitamins and iron and calcium.

Alphatoco Beans
These beans, which look like aduki beans, are offered by seed merchants especially for sprouting. They are particularly rich in vitamin E, are a good source of vitamins C and B and contain a good supply of minerals.

Chick Peas
This bean is very popular in Mediterranean countries where it is made into humous, a delicious purée with .tahini, (sesame seed purée) lemons and garlic, (see page 138). The sprouted bean is rich in vitamin C and contains almost double the iron of most beans and peas.

Flageolet

These are young pale green beans which have a delicate flavour and are delicious sprouted, being eaten either raw or lightly stir-fried with other vegetables. These are one of my favourite beans and contain reasonable amounts of protein, vitamins and minerals.

Lentils

You must buy whole, not split, lentils for sprouting. The common tiny orange lentils are split but when in their whole state they have a brown skin which is removed as the lentils are hulled. These round brown ones have a pleasant nutty flavour when sprouted as do the continental lentils which are brownish/green in colour and flatter in shape. Take care to pick lentils over well not only for broken seeds but for small stones. Sprouted lentils are a good source of protein, contain vitamins A, B, C and E and good amounts of iron, calcium and phosphorous.

Mung Beans

Many people are familiar with these bean sprouts as they are the most commonly sprouted. I love these little green beans sprouted or unsprouted. In India these are sometimes sprouted but are eaten raw or cooked as soon as the tiny shoots appear. These of course will be much more chewy than the Chinese bean sprouts which are sold commercially and used extensively in Chinese cuisine. The Chinese variety are usually 7.5-10 cm/3-4 in long and are plump, crispy and juicy. They are a good source of protein, vitamins and minerals including vitamins A, C and E, iron, calcium and phosphorous.

Soya Beans

These beans, as mentioned in Chapter I, are the most nutritious of all beans, having a complete protein content equal to that of meat (see notes on complete protein page 6). When sprouted the beans are more easily digested and they contain lecithin which helps lower the level of cholesterol in the blood. They are also rich in vitamins A, B, C and E, calcium, iron and phosphorous. They are well worth sprouting, but they need more attention than most sprouting seeds because they ferment quickly. To keep them cool I change the soaking water three times before sprouting then keep them in a cool place. I also rinse them four times daily. But the resulting highly.nutritious sprouted bean is well worth this extra effort.

Sprouting Grains

Barley
Buy pot barley not pearl barley as pearl barley is polished. The sprouted seed is very chewy and best cooked. I toast the sprouted grain and use it in bread-making. The sprouted seeds contain vitamins C, B1 and B2.

Buckwheat
Buckwheat is not a true grain but it's mostly used as one. It contains 11 per cent protein and is rich in iron, the B vitamins and vitamin E. It also contains rutic acid which is known to have a powerful effect on the circulatory system. Do not buy toasted buckwheat as it will not sprout. These sprouts need hulling before eating. To do this simply immerse the sprouted seeds in a bowl of cold water, stir carefully and the hulls will float to the surface. Tilt the bowl and pour off the floating hulls.

Millet
This grain sprouts very easily and is chewy with a sweet taste. I use it in salads and in bread-making to sweeten the loaf. The sprouted seeds are high in protein with good amounts of the B-complex vitamins and calcium. They are often ready within 2 days so are well worth trying.

Wheat

This seed is very easy to sprout and because of its sweetness it is good added to wholemeal flour when baking bread or added to salads to give a sweet taste. Do not over-sprout because they become too tough and are best harvested as soon as the sprout is the same length as the seed. Sprouted wheat contains approximately 14 per cent protein and is well supplied with the B-complex vitamins and vitamin E.

Sprouting Seeds

Alfalfa

The roots of this plant grow to about 12 metres/40 feet or deeper underground, while the plant itself only grows to about 90 cm/3 ft. Experts believe that when plants grow to such depths they gain more minerals from the soil than shallow-growing plants. This plant is regarded in America as a vitally important food supplement. The sprouted seeds contain 40 per cent protein, are rich in vitamins A, B, C, D, E and K and well supplied with calcium, iron, sodium, potassium, sulphur, phosphorous and magnesium. They also have the same amounts of carotene as carrots. The sprouts are very thin and curl around each other in a light bundle. They are excellent in sandwiches.

Fenugreek

You can buy these seeds crushed for tea-making or whole so make sure you buy the latter as the crushed ones will not sprout. These seeds, which are members of the pea family, have a spicy taste and are used extensively in the East in all manner of curry and rice dishes. In medicine, they are considered to be a good cleanser for the liver and kidneys. The leaf of the plant also has a most aromatic spicy taste and is sold as methi. The sprouted seeds contain 30 per cent protein, are rich in vitamins A and C and are a good source of iron.

Sesame Seeds

Buy the unhulled variety as the polished seeds will not sprout. These seeds are a great calcium booster, are high in protein and contain linoleic acid which lowers the level of cholesterol in the blood. They are widely used in Greek and Middle Eastern cuisine and I throw them into any recipe I possibly can including bread, cakes, biscuits, and use them for coating rissoles to mention but a few. The sprouted seeds are full of flavour and are well supplied with vitamins and minerals which include the B-complex and vitamin A, calcium, iron and phosphorous. The sprouts from these seeds are best eaten as soon as the shoots appear as they turn bitter very quickly as they grow.

Sunflower Seeds

These precious seeds are not just for gerbils or hamsters. The sprouted seeds are high in linoleic acid, contain approximately 25 per cent protein, are a rich source of vitamins B, C and E and are well supplied with calcium, iron, magnesium, potassium, phosphorous and zinc. Unlike most seeds you can sprout sunflower seeds in their unhulled state. These are easily obtained from health food or wholefood shops. They should be sprouted in a warmish place.

How to Grow Your own Bean, Grain and Seed Sprouts

To start germinating, all beans and seeds need is the right temperature, water and air. Generally the temperature, which varies depending on the variety of bean or seed you wish to sprout, should be between 18°-21°C/65°-70°F. During the growing period, after the initial soaking, the beans or seeds need to be rinsed regularly but drained well or they will turn sour. They also need air and plenty of space in which to grow. Books on sprouting often advise keeping the growing sprouts in the dark, but I prefer to keep them in the kitchen out of direct sunlight. If grown entirely in the dark they will have more vitamin B2 (Riboflavin) but less vitamin C and no chlorophyll. I sprout mine in the kitchen where they are unlikely to be forgotten.

You will need either a seed sprouter, a kilner or other reasonable size jar, a piece of muslin for the top of the jar and an elastic band.

1. The first step in sprouting is to pick over the chosen beans or seeds and take out any split or crinkled ones and of course remove any stones and bits of sticks. 55 g/2 oz of beans will produce approximately 225 g/8 oz of sprouts. Wash the seeds or beans by placing in a sieve and running cold water over them.
2. Soak the beans or seeds in cold water. The soaking time differs depending on the type of seed you are sprouting so refer to the chart on page 124 which will give you the individual soaking times.
3. If using a seed sprouter follow the manufacturer's directions. If using a jar, drain the soaked beans or seeds. Place in the clear jar and secure the muslin around the opening with an elastic band. Place the jar out of direct sunlight and in a temperature of between 30°-35°C/65°-70°F.

4. The germinating seeds need rinsing at least twice daily but refer to the chart on page 128 for more individual information. Rinse by gently pouring cold water through the muslin, then tipping it and draining all the liquid out again through the muslin. Avoid moving the jar too much as the sprouting beans or seeds are quite delicate and may break and go bad.

Growing Longer Chinese-Style Mung Beans

I have already explained why the commercial mung bean sprouts are longer and straighter than the home-grown variety. Here is a method of achieving home-grown mung bean sprouts more like the commercial ones.

You will need a colander, a polythene bag, tea towel, and a bowl to fit the colander snugly in.

1. Follow directions 1 and 2 for sprouting in a jar.
2. Prick holes with a fork in a good sized polythene bag. Put soaked seeds in bag. Place this in the colander flat. Do not tie up.
3. Dampen the tea towel, fold it and place it over the opening of the plastic bag.
4. Now put the colander snugly into the bowl making sure that there is good drainage space underneath the colander.
5. Place this in a dark place which has a temperature of around 21°-24°C/70°-75°F.
6. Water once every four hours. To do this just lift the colander out of the bowl and pour lukewarm water over the tea towel making sure that all beans or seeds are fed and the water drains away through the holes in the bag and colander. If the beans are not rinsed frequently this method tends to dry them out more quickly. But if you water regularly for about 4-5 days you will end up with sprouts approximately 7.5 cm/3 in long, straight and juicy.
7. To get rid of the green skins, just rinse the grown sprouts in

VARIETY TO BE SPROUTED	Use 2 tablespoons of beans/grains/seeds		
	SOAKING TIME IN HOURS	NUMBER OF DAILY RINSES	SPROUTS READY TO EAT (DAYS)
Beans			
Aduki	12	3	5
Alphatoco	0	3	5
Chick Peas	15	4	4-5
Flageolet	12	3	4
Lentils	8	3	4
Mung Beans	12	3	4-5
Soya Beans	12	4	4-5
Grains			
Barley	12	3	3-4
Buckwheat	12	3	4-5
Millet	12	3	2-3
Wheat	12	3	3
Seeds			
Alfalfa	6	3	5-6
Fenugreek	12	3	4-5
Sesame	8	3	3-4
Sunflower	12	3	4

a large bowl of cold water. Stir a few times and the skins will float to the surface. Pour these away. Drain the sprouts and refrigerate.

Recipes Using Bean, Grain and Seed Sprouts

I mainly use my sprouts in salads because eaten raw they retain all their nutritional qualities. But adding sprouted beans or seeds to the cooking pot need not destroy all the nutrients if care is taken in the way the dish is prepared. They will not only enhance your meals with varied flavours and textures, but they will supply more nutrients than if used in their dormant state.

I will start this recipe section with ideas for incorporating particular bean or seed sprouts into some of the recipes from other chapters in the book. This will show you the versatility there is in making your own home proteins when a similar mixture of vegetables, grains and sauces can so easily accompany a variety of different proteins. For example if you have no tofu for the Tofu Risotto recipe on pages 25–6 try the following recipe.

Sprouted Aduki Bean Risotto

See recipe for Tofu Risotto on pages 25–6.

Substitute 285 g/10 oz sprouted aduki beans for the tofu and see how they complement the Rich Italian Sauce. When you get to stage 5 in the method for the sauce, cook the sprouted aduki beans in it for 5 minutes only then stir in the rice. It's as simple as that.

Mung Bean Sprouts with
Sweet and Sour Sauce

See recipe for Tofu Tempura with Sweet and Sour Sauce, on pages 27–9 and substitute 285 g/10 oz sprouted mung beans (long length) for the tofu. Simply add the bean sprouts with the peppers at stage 2 in the method for making the sauce and continue to stage 5 only. Serve with plain boiled Surinam rice.

Tabbouleh (Bulgur Wheat Salad) with
Sprouted Sesame or Sunflower Seeds

See recipe for Tempeh Tabbouleh on pages 51–2. Substitute 180 g/6 oz sprouted sesame or sunflower seeds for the tempeh. Leave out the pine nuts. When you get to stage 6 in the method just stir the sprouted seeds into the bulgur mixture and garnish with watercress only.

Italian Mango Curry Soup with
Sprouted Lentils

See recipe for Indian Mango Curry Soup with tempeh on page 57. Substitute 225 g/8 oz sprouted lentils for the tempeh and add these just 10 minutes before the end of cooking time.

Ratatouille with Sprouted Millet

See recipe for Ratatouille with Tempeh on page 60. Omit the tempeh and sprout 115 g/4 oz dry weight of millet. This takes just 2 to 3 days and the sprout must be harvested as soon as it is just a very little bit longer than the grain. Cook the sauce as directed and turn into an ovenproof dish. Sprinkle over the sprouted millet. Top with 115 g/4 oz grated Cheddar cheese and put under a grill on medium heat until golden brown.

Sprouted Aduki Bean Moussaka

See recipe for Moussaka with Minced Gluten on pages 77–8. Substitute 285 g/10 oz of sprouted aduki beans (short length: see chart on page 124). At stage 4 in the method just omit the gluten and stir in the aduki sprouts. When they have simmered in the onion and tomato mixture for 7 minutes, mash them with a potato masher and proceed with the rest of the method.

Sprouted Soya Beans with Chilli Sauce

See recipe for Chilli Beans with Minced Gluten on page 79. Substitute 340 g/12 oz sprouted soya beans (short length, see chart on page 124) for the kidney beans and gluten balls. Steam the short sprouted soya beans for 20 minutes. Add these to the chilli sauce at stage 6 in the method.

Sprouted Flageolet Beans with Spiced Mushroom and Tomato Sauce

See recipe for Paneer (lemon cheese) with Spiced Mushrooms, Tomato and Green Pea Sauce, on pages 97–8. Substitute 285 g/10 oz sprouted flageolet beans for the frozen peas and omit the paneer. Start method at no. 3 and add the sprouts at stage 9 with the mushrooms.

Here are a few more recipes to add to these adaptations.

Chinese Sweet and Sour Salad with
Mung Bean Sprouts
Serves 4

285 g/10 oz sprouted mung beans
1 small bunch spring onions, finely chopped (use green ends)
1 medium carrot, cut in very thin slanting ovals
1 small red or green pepper, finely chopped
55 g/2 oz small button mushrooms, thinly sliced
2 slices of pineapple, fresh or canned, cut in small chunks

For the Dressing

4 tablespoons sesame or safflower oil
1 tablespoon cider vinegar or lemon juice
1 tablespoon shoyu (naturally fermented soya sauce)
1 level teaspoon clear honey
¼ teaspoon dry mustard
pinch of five spice or allspice
1 teaspoon freshly grated root ginger
1 clove garlic, crushed

Combine the salad ingredients in a serving bowl. Shake up the ingredients in a screw-top jar and pour over the salad 10 minutes before needed. This will give time for the salad vegetables to absorb the flavours of the dressing. Toss again in the dressing just before serving.

Sprouted Chick Pea and Olive
Salad Vinaigrette
Serves 4

285 g/10 oz sprouted chick peas
8 black olives, stoned and halved
5 firm tomatoes, cut in thin wedges
1 small green pepper, cut in thin slices then quartered
2 bunches watercress

2 small eggs, hard-boiled, and
 sliced
1 small onion, cut in thin rings

1 tablespoon fresh chopped mint
 leaves

Vinaigrette Dressing

4 tablespoons olive oil or
 sunflower oil
1 ½ tablespoons lemon juice
¼ teaspoon mustard powder
¼ teaspoon freshly ground black

pepper
½ teaspoon sea salt
½ teaspoon honey (optional)
1 large clove garlic

1. Make the dressing and shake well in a screw-top jar.
2. Place chick peas and olives in a bowl and pour on half the dressing. Mix well in.
3. Fork in the tomato wedges and the green pepper.
4. Wash watercress and break into small sprigs.
5. To assemble the salad, spread the watercress sprigs on the bottom of a shallow serving bowl, spoon on the chick pea mixture, and garnish the top with the hard-boiled egg slices and the onion rings. Pour over the remaining dressing and sprinkle on the chopped mint.

Sprouted Flageolet Beans
with Avocado Dressing
Serves 4

This makes a lively, tasty starter and looks delightful with its varied shades of green.

285 g/10 oz sprouted flageolet
 beans
1 crisp green lettuce

a little finely chopped parsley to
 garnish

For the Avocado Dressing

55 g/2 oz either tofu or Soya
  yoghurt cheese, see pages 13–16
  and 19–20 respectively
½ good sized avocado
1 large clove garlic
1 tablespoon olive oil

2 tablespoons lemon juice
1 teaspoon Dijon mustard
½ teaspoon clear honey (optional)
sea salt and freshly ground black
  pepper

1. Wash the lettuce and break off whole leaves.
2. Place sprouted beans in a mixing bowl.
3. Liquidise all the avocado dressing ingredients together in a blender or food processor.
4. Stir the dressing into the sprouted flageolet beans. Now spoon the dressed beans into the individual lettuce leaves and garnish each with a little chopped parsley.

Sprouted Lentil Salad with Tamarind Dressing
Serves 4

You can buy tamarind in Indian grocery shops and in health food stores. It looks like pressed dates and has to be soaked in water then passed through a sieve to remove the stone-like seeds. It is often used in curry sauces and has a citrus flavour. Watch out for the stone-like seeds.

340 g/12 oz sprouted·brown or
  continental lentils
4 tomatoes, cut in wedges

½ small cucumber, cut in small
  chunks
1 small onion, very finely chopped

For the Tamarind Dressing

30 g/1 oz tamarind
1 very level teaspoon curry powder
3 tablespoons sunflower oil
small clove garlic, crushed

½ teaspoon clear honey
2 generous tablespoons natural
  yoghurt
little sea salt to taste

1. In a serving bowl, combine the sprouted lentils with the tomatoes, cucumber and onion.
2. Soak the tamarind in 3 tablespoons boiling water and the curry powder for 10 minutes.
3. Pass through a sieve. You will have a thickish brown liquid. Blend this with the dressing ingredients and stir into the sprouted lentil mixture.

This is delicious either served as a starter or as an accompaniment to a vegetable or meat curry.

Saffron Rice with Sprouted Sesame or Sunflower Seeds and Shoyu Dressing
Serves 4

1 large onion
1 large clove garlic
2 tablespoons sunflower oil
225 g/8 oz short or long grain Italian brown rice
575 ml/1 pint boiling water
1 vegetable stock cube or level teaspoon sea salt

pinch of Saffron or 1 level teaspoon turmeric
225 g/8 oz frozen peas cooked for 4 minutes only
170 g/6 oz sprouted sesame or sunflower seeds
a little chopped parsley to garnish

For the Shoyu Dressing

4 tablespoons sunflower oil
3 tablespoons cider vinegar
1 small clove garlic
¼ teaspoon mustard powder

½ teaspoon clear honey (optional)
3 teaspoons shoyu (naturally fermented soya sauce)

1. In a heavy-based medium sized saucepan sauté onion and garlic in 2 tablespoons sunflower oil for 10 minutes with lid on.
2. Wash the rice by placing in a sieve and letting cold water run through the grains. Drain well and add to sautéed onion and garlic. Fry gently for 4 minutes.

3. Pour in the boiling water (to which the saffron has been added) and stock cube or sea salt. Bring to boil and simmer gently with the lid on for 30 to 35 minutes. When cooked, the rice should have absorbed all the liquid. Add the peas.
4. Blend all dressing ingredients together and shake in a screw-top jar.
5. Put cooked rice in a serving bowl and stir in the dressing. Then fork in the sesame or sunflower sprouts and garnish with a little chopped parsley.

This is delicious served hot or cold.

Leeks and Mushrooms with Soya Bean Sprouts

This is a very simple and quite delicious mixture.

225 g/8 oz sprouted soya beans
2 large sized leeks, washed, trimmed and cut into .6 cm/¼ in rings, using soft green ends as well
115 g/4 oz small button

mushrooms
1 scant tablespoon shoyu (naturally fermented soya sauce)
a little freshly ground black pepper

1. Steam the sprouted soya beans for 5 minutes.
2. Sauté the leeks in the oil for 5 minutes.
3. Add the mushrooms and the sprouts and continue to sauté for 5 minutes more.
4. Stir in the shoyu and black pepper.

I serve this mixture in several ways which are all greatly enjoyed. It can be used as a vegetable accompaniment for four, a substantial lunch or supper dish for two with wholemeal toast or to feed six hungry people in the following two recipes.

Leek, Mushroom and Sprouted Soya Bean Stuffed Pancakes

*1 quantity Leeks and Mushrooms
with Soya Bean Sprouts
1 quantity Parsley Pancakes (see
pages 65–6)
675 ml/1 ¼ pints milk
55 g/2 oz unbleached flour
a little mustard powder*

*85-115 g/3-4 oz grated cheese
(reserve a little to sprinkle
on top)
freshly ground black pepper and
sea salt
pinch of dried tarragon*

1. To make the sauce, heat 1 pint of the milk to just under boiling point. Mix the other ¼ pint of milk with the flour, mustard powder, pepper and salt. Pour on the heated milk and cook for 1 minute. Take off the heat and stir in the grated cheese.
2. Stuff each pancake with the leek and sprout mixture.
3. Pour the sauce over the pancakes, sprinkle on the cheese and bake at 190°C/375°F/Gas 5 for 15 minutes. Brown under a grill.

Leek, Mushroom and Sprouted Soya Bean Quiche

Another simple way to feed six using the recipe for Leeks and Mushrooms with Soya Bean Sprouts. It is a high protein dish and fills a 25 cm/10 in flan dish.

*1 quantity Wholemeal Pastry case
baked blind (see pages 35–6)
1 quantity Leeks and Mushrooms
with Soya Bean Sprouts (see
page 132), but leave out the
shoyu
3 eggs
2 tablespoons natural yoghurt
180 ml/6 fl oz milk*

*1 rounded tablespoon dried milk
powder
¼ teaspoon ground mace
¼ teaspoon mustard
sea salt and freshly ground black
pepper to taste
a little oregano
85 g/3 oz Cheddar cheese,
grated*

1. When pastry case is cool sprinkle 55 g/2 oz of the cheese on the base.
2. Spoon on the leek mixture when it is cool.
3. Whisk eggs with milk, yoghurt, milk powder, mace, mustard, sea salt and freshly ground black pepper. Pour this over the leek mixture and sprinkle the 30 g/1 oz cheese and a little oregano on top.
4. Bake at 190°C/375°F/Gas 5 for 35 to 40 minutes.

In the short chapter which follows you will find sprouted seeds in the high protein loaf and some spreads or dips which include sprouted beans and seeds.

APPENDIX
❧ *Nutritious Sandwich Fillers* ❧

You can make a most exciting variety of spreads and pâtés from beans, nuts and seeds, dairy produce and vegetables when you purée these foods with dried herbs and spices.

The following recipes, preceded by a high protein loaf, can be used as wholesome sandwich fillers or as party dips.

High-Protein Loaf

This recipe will make four loaves which will fit 450 g/1 lb tins, although they will weigh more than 450 g/1 lb.

1.4 kg/3 lb stoneground wholemeal flour
85 g/3 oz soya flour
30 g/1 oz wheatgerm
115 g/4 oz sprouted sesame seeds or sunflower seeds
30 g/1 oz dried yeast or 55 g/2 oz fresh yeast

1 level tablespoon sea salt
just under 1 litre/1 ¾ pints warm water
about 2 teaspoons molasses
1 tablespoon malt extract
2 tablespoons corn or sunflower oil
a little beaten egg and 1 teaspoon sesame seeds for top of loaves

1. Mix the flour, salt and sesame seeds in a warm bowl and keep warm. Measure out the required warm water in a large jug. Take out 275 ml/½ pint to which you add the yeast and ¼ teaspoon of the molasses. Stir and leave to froth in a warm place for 5-7 minutes.

2. Add the malt extract, oil and 1 heaped teaspoon molasses to the remaining warm water and stir.
3. When the yeast liquid is frothy add this and the malted liquid to the flour mixture by making a well in the middle and gradually working it into a soft dough. At this stage remember to leave some of the malted liquid in the jug so that you can be sure not to make the dough too wet. Flours differ in texture and absorb different amounts of liquid.
4. Knead the dough for 7 minutes then place it in a greased polythene bag, leaving room for it to rise. Wrap in a warm towel and leave to rise for 45 minutes to 1 hour then knock back and knead for 1 minute. It is now ready to use.
5. Cut the dough into four and form into loaves.
6. Brush with beaten egg and sprinkle with sesame seeds. Place in the prepared loaf tins and leave to rise in a warm, draught-free place for 20 minutes covered with a damp cloth. Bake in a preheated oven on the middle shelf at 230°C/450°F/Gas 8 for 10 minutes then at 190°C/375°F/Gas 5 for 25 minutes. Cool for 10 minutes in the tin and turn the bread out onto a wire rack.

Avocado and Soft Cheese Spread

1 good sized avocado, stoned and chopped
115 g/4 oz Sally's Soft Cheese or Lactic Curd Cheese, (see pages 92–3 and 90–1)
1 clove garlic
few drops of Tabasco sauce (optional)
little sea salt
1 small red pepper, very finely chopped

1. Blend avocado with garlic and the Lactic Curd or Soft Cheese, in a blender or food processor.
2. Stir in the remaining ingredients by hand.

This is great as a dip or a sandwich filler with crisp lettuce leaves.

Sprouted Soya Bean Spread

The sprouted beans have to be cooked for 1 hour to achieve a smooth purée.

170 g/6 oz dry weight soya beans, sprouted
2 large cloves of garlic
4 tablespoons fresh chopped parsley
juice of about 1 lemon

2 tablespoons cold pressed sunflower oil
sea salt and freshly ground black pepper to taste

1. Cook the sprouted soya beans until soft, about 1 hour.
2. Purée all ingredients in a food processor until smooth.

Soya Bean and Sprouted Sesame Seed Spread

170 g/6 oz dry weight soya beans
2 tablespoons cold pressed sunflower oil
3 tablespoons lemon juice
6 spring onions, very finely chopped using green ends
3 tablespoons green pepper, very finely chopped

115 g/4 oz sprouted sesame seeds
2 tablespoons fresh parsley, chopped
1 tablespoon shoyu (naturally fermented soya sauce)
sea salt and freshly ground black pepper to taste

1. Soak the beans for at least 16 hours changing the water 3 times. Rinse and cook in fresh water for 3 hours until soft. (Pressure cook for 30 minutes.) Add sea salt 10 minutes before end of cooking time.
2. Drain beans and purée with the oil and lemon juice until smooth.
3. Stir in all other ingredients with a fork.

Humous (Purée of Chick Peas)

This beautiful purée originates from the Middle East and is delicious as a filler for pitta bread with crisp fresh lettuce.

225 g/8 oz dry chick peas
sea salt
juice of 2 lemons
2 tablespoons tahini (sesame seed paste)
2 cloves garlic

2 tablespoons olive oil
sea salt and freshly ground black pepper
1 tablespoon fresh mint
crisp lettuce leaves, to serve

1. Wash the peas and pick over for stones.
2. Soak peas for at least 12 hours changing the water three times. Rinse and cook in 1.1 litres/2 pints water for 1 hour or until soft. Add 1 tablespoon sea salt 10 minutes before end of cooking time.
3. Blend the peas and lemon juice, tahini, garlic and olive oil using either a blender or a food processor until you have a thick, creamy consistency. It may be necessary to add a little of the cooking water to achieve a smooth purée.
4. Place in a serving bowl and add sea salt and freshly ground black pepper to taste.

Garnish with a sprig of mint. Serve on crisp lettuce leaves.

Toasted Nut and Seed Pâté

You can use any variety of nuts and seeds, but this mixture is particularly delicious.

340 g/12 oz mixed nuts and seeds (almonds, hazelnuts, cashews, sunflower, pumpkin and sesame seeds)

6 tablespoons cold pressed sunflower oil
1 small onion, peeled and roughly chopped

½ small red and ½ small green
  pepper
1 tablespoon shoyu (naturally
  fermented soya sauce)
1 teaspoon sweet mixed herbs

140 ml/¼ pint thick natural
  yoghurt
freshly ground black pepper to
  taste

1. Toast the nuts and seeds in a heavy-based pan on moderate heat turning constantly with a wooden spoon until lightly roasted (about 10 minutes).
2. Using an electric blender or food processor blend the nuts with the cold pressed oil until nearly smooth. (The texture is up to you – the longer you process, the smoother the pâté.)
3. Scoop out and place in a serving bowl.
4. Put onion, red and green pepper, shoyu and mixed herbs into the blender or processor and blend until puréed.
5. Stir the purée with the yoghurt into the ground nuts and seeds. Taste and add freshly ground black pepper and a little more shoyu if you wish.

Delicious as a dip, this is also wonderfully nutritious as a tasty sandwich filler.

ᐧ§ *Useful Addresses* §ᐤ

Tofu, firm and silken Nigari Tofu Press	Paul's Tofu The Old Brewery Wheathampstead House Wheathampstead St Albans Hertfordshire 058 283 4241
Tempeh culture	Micro Audit Ltd Wheathampstead House Wheathampstead St Albans Hertfordshire 058 283 2370
Dairy thermometer Cheese press	Astell Laboratories Service Co. 172 Brownhill Road London SE6 2DL
Information and books	Goat Society Rougham Bury St Edmunds Suffolk
Animal and vegetable rennet Cheese culture	Christian Hansen Laboratories Ltd, 467 Basingstoke Road Reading RG2 0QL Berkshire

Index